The Essence of
The Economy

The Essence of Management Series

The Essence of Marketing
The Essence of Marketing Research
The Essence of Industrial Marketing
The Essence of International Marketing
The Essence of Services Marketing
The Essence of Financial Accounting
The Essence of Management Accounting
The Essence of Financial Management
The Essence of International Money
The Essence of Mergers and Acquisitions
The Essence of Organizational Behaviour
The Essence of Industrial Relations and Personnel Management
The Essence of Women in Management
The Essence of the Economy
The Essence of Business Economics
The Essence of International Business
The Essence of Personal Microcomputing
The Essence of Information Systems
The Essence of Operations Management
The Essence of Strategic Management
The Essence of Business Law
The Essence of Entrepreneurship and New Ventures
The Essence of Venture Capital and Buy-outs
The Essence of Small Business
The Essence of Recruitment and Selection
The Essence of Effective Communication
The Essence of Statistics for Business

The Essence of The Economy

Joseph G. Nellis

Senior Lecturer in Business Economics
Cranfield School of Management

and

David Parker

Senior Lecturer in Business Economics
Cranfield School of Management

Prentice Hall

New York   London   Toronto   Sydney   Tokyo   Singapore

First published 1990 by
Prentice Hall International (UK) Ltd
Campus 400, Maylands Avenue
Hemel Hempstead
Hertfordshire HP2 7EZ
A division of
Simon & Schuster International Group

© Prentice Hall International (UK) Ltd, 1990

Typeset in 11/12 pt Palatino
by Key Graphics, Aldermaston, Berkshire

Printed and bound in Great Britain by
BPC Wheatons Ltd, Exeter

British Library Cataloguing in Publication Data

Nellis, J. G.
    Essence of the economy. – (The essence of management
series).
    1. Economics
I. Title   II. Parker, David   III. Series
330

    ISBN 0-13-284696-9

Library of Congress Cataloging-in-Publication Data

Nellis, J. G.
    The Essence of the economy / by Joseph G. Nellis and David Parker.
        p.   cm. — (The Essence of management series)
    Includes bibliographical references (p.) and index.
    ISBN 0-13-284696-9
    1. United States—Economic conditions—1981–   2. Economics.
I. Parker, David.   II. Title.   III. Series.
HC106.8.N44   1990   330 – dc20   90-14164
                                            CIP

---

10 9 8 7 6 98 97 96 95 94

To
Helen, Gareth and Daniel
Megan, Michael and Matthew

Contents

Preface

As the world of business becomes more competitive, more dynamic and more global, there is a growing and indeed urgent need for managers to be critically aware of the events taking place in their wider economic environment. 'No business is an island' and, consequently, no manager can afford to ignore the importance of changes in the external economic conditions under which commerce and business must take place. Those conditions are not always friendly – think about the boardroom panic (to varying degrees) when headlines report increases in interest rates, inflation and taxes, or the unsteadiness of sterling. The reason for this panic is simply explained by the fact that events such as these are beyond the control of boardroom members and managers. Companies may feel they are in control of more domestic (i.e. internal) matters such as pricing policy, production levels, marketing expenditure, R&D, etc., but it is an inescapable fact that no company is able to control its external economic environment; and ultimately it is changes in the external environment that cause the death of many companies.

Recognizing the importance of the external economy on business decision making is one thing; responding to it is quite a different matter. To be able to reach sound business decisions in a dynamic economy requires managers to have a clear understanding of economic interrelationships and their impact upon business. For example, if interest rates go up, what is likely to happen to exchange rates, consumer spending, savings, prices etc., and what will be the consequence for businesses? Or, if the balance of payments on current account collapses, what are the likely implications for the exchange rate, interest rates, taxes, etc., and ultimately, economic growth?

The aim of this book is to provide a clear and concise picture of the way in which an economy works and why different governments adopt different economic policies. This is not a book for those with a specialist interest in economics; it is a book for those interested in the economy in the widest possible sense. In particular, since every business is directly affected by economic events, every manager should find this book useful. In addition, since economics is a compulsory element in many professional management courses, participants on such courses should find the book attractive, including those on Master of Business Administration (MBA) and Diploma in Management Studies (DMS) programmes as well as practising managers attending continuing studies courses in which the economic environment of business is an integral part. The book is also suitably structured for students attending business studies and general economics courses at universities, polytechnics and colleges of further and higher education. More generally, the book is intended to provide a 'communication bridge' between managers and professional economists, and to this end we have avoided as far as possible the use of inaccessible jargon and esoteric debate.

We are indebted to our secretary, Christine Williams, for typing the various drafts of the manuscript. Again, she has amazed us by maintaining her joviality when confronted with two authors for whom the deadline for work was always yesterday. We are also grateful to our colleagues, Dr Frank Fishwick and Professor Adrian Buckley, for their advice and many helpful suggestions during the writing of the book. Thanks are also due to those students and managers who have attended Cranfield School of Management in recent years. Their contributions to classroom discussions were invaluable both in encouraging us to write this book and, perhaps more importantly, in helping us to focus on the key issues and topics.

Lastly, we are thankful to our families for their support. This book has in every sense been a joint effort, and it is dedicated to them.

Joseph G. Nellis
David Parker
Cranfield School of Management

1

The essence of the economy:
An overview

Business and the economy

The success or failure of a business is, to a large extent, dependent upon how its managers perform in terms of financial controls, marketing strategies, product design, research and development, etc. A great deal of time and effort is spent by successful firms in ensuring that the right decisions are made in a competitive environment with the greatest attention being paid to the immediate environment in which the firms are operating – to the workforce, to the production line, to the marketplace for products, to direct competitors. This immediate environment is described as the *microeconomic* environment of a firm and involves prices, revenues, costs, employment levels and so on.

There are, however, other facets of a firm's environment of which the most notable comprise the general social and economic conditions of the larger system of which each firm forms a part. Changing social values (for example, with regard to the natural environment) combined with social movements powerfully condition economic activity and, hence, the way in which companies are operated by the managers and workers within them. The political and legal frameworks of a country also have a significant

1

impact upon the business sector and the way in which firms attempt to carry out their activities. Inevitably, in this book our attention will be focused mainly on the more direct economic facets of the firm's wider environment, that is the *macroeconomy*. In contrast to the microeconomy, this refers to the factors which are external to the immediate environment of the firm: it involves changes in general inflation and employment, for example, rather than changes in the firm's own product prices and workforce. Macroeconomics, therefore, refers to the aggregate national and, increasingly, international economy of which the firm is a subunit.

By definition, since each firm is a subunit of the larger economic system, it is unable to exercise control over the macroeconomic environment in the way that it has control (though perhaps limited) over its microeconomic environment. Yet, a plain truth stares every firm in the face: failure to adapt to a changing, dynamic macroeconomy inevitably results in business failure. Nevertheless, how many managers actively seek to keep themselves informed of the key developments within the wider economy? How many managers actively seek to monitor and forecast wider economic trends and plan investment and production accordingly? One thing is certain: successful firms pay infinitely more attention to these external economic factors than those firms that struggle to survive. Ultimately, the changing macroeconomy determines growth in the nation's income and its ability to expand demand for products. Far too many managers 'keep their heads down', making sure that the day-to-day things are going smoothly. Day-to-day things are important but success requires critical awareness and a vision of future economic prospects.

The aim in this book is to provide managers with the basic skills and understanding of the macroeconomy upon which they can build this critical awareness and vision. There are, of course, no simple right or wrong answers: instead, we hope to build a foundation of understanding and enthusiasm to learn more about the way in which the macroeconomy operates and the impact it has upon the business world in order to assist managers in their decision making.

In this chapter the scene is set for the discussion of the wider economic environment and analysis of economic principles and policy in subsequent chapters. In particular, we outline the major economic problems facing countries like the UK today and the different policy measures that governments can adopt to tackle these problems. We also consider the nature of the economic problem which lies at the heart of the study of economics and introduce the concept of opportunity cost. Lastly, we present a brief overview of the role of government in the economy. The precise degree to which governments need to involve themselves in managing the economy is a recurring debate in economics.

Introducing the macroeconomic environment of business

It is not difficult to identify which aspects of the macroeconomic environment are of greatest importance to business decision making: *all* aspects are important. This is readily confirmed by asking a group of managers to decide whether or not changes in each of the following macroeconomic variables are likely to have an impact upon their businesses (recognizing that some variables will have a more immediate and direct impact than others):

Economic growth.

Inflation.

Interest rates.

Availability of credit and monetary growth.

Total investment.

Public expenditure plans.

Taxation, personal and corporate.

Total consumer expenditure.

Total savings.

Wages and earnings at the economy level.

Employment trends.

Imports, exports and the balance of payments.

The list could be extended considerably but the message is that firms operate within an environment that is extremely complex and dynamic.

In addition, all of these economic variables are interrelated to some extent. For example, changes in monetary growth affect interest rates; changes in taxation have implications for the level of public expenditure as well as consumer spending and investment. Furthermore, all of these variables are either directly controlled by the government or indirectly affected by government economic policies. These policies may be summarized under the general headings of:

Fiscal policy

Monetary policy.

Figure 1.1 The business environment.

Exchange rate policy.

International trade policy.

Supply-side policy.

Prices and incomes policy.

Employment policy.

The extent to which firms are vulnerable to both domestic and international macroeconomic factors is summarized in Figure 1.1.

Fiscal policy

Fiscal policy is concerned with the composition of and changes in the levels of public expenditure and taxation. Changes in the UK are generally announced once a year. Public expenditure figures for the current fiscal year (1 April to 31 March) and targets for the following three years are published in the government's Autumn Financial Statement usually released in November and in the public expenditure White Paper the following January, while changes in the level and structure of taxation (personal and corporate) are announced in the Chancellor of the Exchequer's budget speech in March which introduces into Parliament the annual Finance Bill.

Monetary policy

Monetary policy is defined as government measures to influence the cost (i.e. the rate of interest) and availability of credit in the economy thereby affecting the overall supply of money. While fiscal changes are announced annually or at other intervals, monetary policy measures are continuous. For example, the government may announce interest rate changes at any time, and these rapidly affect the level and structure of competing interest rates generally (such as building society mortgage rates).

Exchange rate policy

Exchange rate policy refers to government intervention on the foreign exchange markets to influence the level and direction of the external value of a country's currency. The degree of intervention depends upon the government's specific exchange rate objective: whether to have a fixed, freely floating or managed rate and, where the exchange rate is fixed or managed, at what level to 'peg' the rate. Exchange rate policy has important implications for trade and capital flows in and out of the country, i.e. for the balance of payments. It also has an impact upon domestic monetary policy since interest rate levels may have to be set to protect the exchange rate by influencing international capital flows.

International trade policy

Trade policy involves measures taken by government, in addition to exchange rate policy, to influence the magnitude and direction of foreign trade. There may be many reasons for these measures, notably correction of balance of payments problems, preserving domestic employment, encouraging economic growth and promoting foreign co-operation (for example, within the European Community). The measures may take the form of subsidies for exports, tariffs (duties) on imports and other protectionist measures such as import quotas.

Supply-side policy

Supply-side policy arises out of what is often termed supply-side economics. It refers to those government policies that are directed at tackling problems involving the aggregate supply (i.e. production) of goods and services in the economy. Supply-side policy, therefore, contrasts with the policies described above, especially fiscal and monetary policies, which are concerned with affecting the level of total or aggregate demand for goods and services. Measures used are directed specifically at influencing productivity and output costs. These may involve the introduction of new technology, the encouragement of competition and enterprise, privatization of state assets, efforts to increase labour efficiency and other measures to improve the operation of the market economy.

Prices and incomes policies

Prices and incomes policies are examples of direct intervention by government in the working of a market economy. They involve government intervention in the setting of prices for goods and services and in influencing wage settlements. These policies have two fundamental aims: control over general inflation and the protection of jobs in the domestic economy. In addition, prices and incomes policies can have a significant impact upon the distribution of income. There is a general view among economists, however, that prices and incomes policies should be regarded only as temporary or emergency measures: they distort the operation of markets by undermining wage and price levels which reflect the demand for and supply of goods, services and labour.

Employment policy

Employment policy is concerned with government efforts to create jobs and thereby reduce unemployment. The policy may be implemented either indirectly, via stimulation of aggregate demand in the economy, or directly through job creation schemes and training programmes.

Clearly, there is a large degree of overlap between these various policies and their impact upon the macroeconomic variables listed earlier. These interrelationships are stressed throughout the book. We now consider the overriding economic problem that faces governments, individuals and firms and from which the study of economics has evolved.

The economic problem

At the heart of the study of economics is the problem of how countries attempt to match the demands on their resources with the available supply. Despite a phenomenal growth in production since the Industrial Revolution, there is no evidence that, even in the richest countries, people's wants are satisfied. Although most people in the industrialized world are well fed, clothed and housed, new wants are continuously being created: the high street is crowded with people wanting the latest fashions and electronic gadgets. Even the nature of the desirable home has changed. Thirty years ago house buyers in Britain looked for inside lavatories, but today they increasingly seek en-suite bathrooms and double garages. At the same time, however, for over one-half of the world's population – those in developing countries – life remains harsh. Here, basic sanitation replaces the en-suite bathroom as a priority want. Indeed, in these countries there remains a desperate need for the most basic of foodstuffs and other necessities of life to ward off malnutrition and disease.

The message is clear enough: wants are limitless but the resources to satisfy them are scarce. Therefore, all societies – from the richest to the poorest – share a common economic problem involving the allocation of scarce resources to meet the needs and demands of consumers and producers. How should resources be allocated when satisfying one set of wants inevitably means another set is not met? This is equally true for individuals, firms and governments, who all face the same kind of economic problem. The individual who buys a larger house may have to forgo the annual foreign holiday. The firm that pays more to its workforce may have to reduce its investment in new plant. When the government buys more school books out of the education budget, there may be a shortage of money available to employ teachers. In other words, every decision

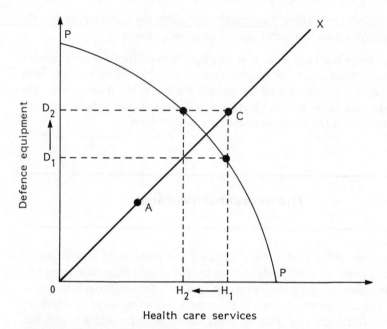

Figure 1.2 Production possibility curve.

involving the satisfaction of wants using scarce resources involves a choice. Each use of resources means forgoing some other use.

When discussing resource use, economists use the term *opportunity cost* to describe the next best option forgone. The concept of opportunity cost can be usefully illustrated in a simple diagram. The curve PP in Figure 1.2 represents what is called a *production possibility curve* (PPC) or *frontier*. It tells us the maximum output of two goods or services that can be obtained given the current level of resources and assuming maximum efficiency in production (the idea can be extended to any number of goods or services though only two can be neatly represented on a two-dimensional diagram). The latter assumption means that resources are not wasted in producing the goods and services. To illustrate the concept of opportunity cost, assume that the two goods are defence equipment and health care services. It should be appreciated that if there are no more resources available, then to produce one unit more of something means producing less of another good (there is an opportunity cost). Therefore, if a country should decide to raise defence spending and obtain more defence equipment then the curve shows that this can be achieved only by reducing the resources used in providing health care.

The increase in defence spending is represented by a shift from point

D_1 to D_2 and the fall in spending upon the health sector as a movement from point H_1 to H_2 in Figure 1.2. The reduced output of health care is the opportunity cost of achieving more defence equipment. Similar trade-offs between defence equipment and health care are shown anywhere along the PPC curve. The shape of the curve, incidentally, reflects the fact that as we transfer more and more resources from one use to another – health care to defence equipment or vice versa – the resulting increase in output (of defence spending in this case) is likely to decline. This relates to the concept of *diminishing marginal returns*. It states that as we apply more of one input (e.g. labour) to another input (e.g. capital or land) then after some point the resulting increase in output becomes smaller and smaller. Therefore, for example, equal amounts of resources removed from the defence industry and employed in health care produce an increasingly smaller addition to the health care output.

It should be noted that since the PPC curve shows the maximum production of defence equipment and health care possible with the available resources, any production combination below the curve (e.g. point A) represents an inefficient use of resources. In contrast, any point above the curve, which of course we should prefer since it implies we can have both more health care and defence equipment (e.g. point C), cannot be achieved given the current level of the country's economic resources. The obvious solution to the trade-off between defence and health care as implied by the PPC is to increase the capacity of the economy to produce more of both. This is what is meant by *economic growth* and would be illustrated by an outward shift of the PPC. One objective of government, therefore, is to stimulate economic growth and hence raise economic welfare by moving the economy along a growth path such as OX. Whether governments should attempt to do this by active intervention in the economy (e.g. through planning and investment subsidies), or whether they should simply maintain an economic and political environment in which private enterprise can flourish, continues to divide economists, much as it has done for centuries.

Government and the economy

All societies face the economic problem outlined above but they may attempt to solve it in different ways. One approach is to have a central planning body which makes all of the decisions about whose wants will be met and how. The Soviet Union is a good example of a planned economy since the war. In the Soviet Union, resource use has been directed through a powerful hierarchy of state agencies headed by the USSR State Planning Committee (called Gosplan). Along with the Ministry of Finance and around nine hundred ministries and departments scattered across the Soviet Union, Gosplan has controlled the entire national economy of that country. The planners have decided what to produce, how the goods and services should be supplied, where production should take place and to whom the goods and services should be distributed.

An alternative approach, more favoured in the West and recently encouraged in the Soviet bloc under President Gorbachev and his programme of *perestroika* is reliance on the price or market system. In the West this takes the form of the capitalist system, a system which is associated with the private ownership of resources. Instead of the allocation of resources through central planning, a capitalist economy uses prices as a signal to both producers and consumers operating in the free market. Prices indicate what and how much firms should produce to maximize their profits and they regulate how much consumers should buy to satisfy their wants. If a price is set too low, demand will exceed supply and prices will therefore tend to rise. In contrast, if a price is set too high supply will exceed demand and prices will be forced down.

In this way the price mechanism allocates resources according to consumer demand reflected in the prices that consumers are willing to pay. A major objection to capitalism, however, is unfairness in the distribution of resources, and it is this which led to the rise of socialism as a political and economic alternative to capitalism in the nineteenth century. In the free market economy, those with the highest incomes have more influence on the distribution of resources than those on low incomes. Each pound spent in the marketplace acts like a vote for goods and services. Those with the largest incomes and wealth therefore have the largest number of votes. This is not an equal 'franchise' so, therefore, central planning in which everyone (in principle) receives a more equal amount would seem fairer. In practice, however, it has often been associated with waste and poor quality; i.e. producing well inside the production possibility curve in Figure 1.2. For example, the Soviet Union produces two-and-a-half times more shoes than the USA but shortages of footwear continue. The shoes produced are of poor quality and do not last long. Wasting economic resources is equivalent to moving the production possibility curve in Figure 1.2 inwards towards the origin – fewer of all goods are produced and economic well-being declines.

In practice, all economies fall somewhere between the two extremes of central planning and completely free capitalist markets. They are known, therefore, as *mixed economies*. In the Soviet Union, while most resources have been allocated by the state, there remains a small market sector. In contrast, in the USA (generally recognized as the leading capitalist economy) there is considerable state involvement in the provision of welfare services, law and order, and defence. In all capitalist economies, governments aim to varying degrees to make the 'votes' in the marketplace more equal through taxation and welfare benefits. The extent to which this should and can be done, however, without creating economic disincentives remains controversial.

There are many reasons why governments may want to intervene in markets, even in capitalist economies. These come under a number of headings relating to:

Provision of essential services.

Transfer payments.

Natural monopolies.

Social costs and benefits.

Support for industry and commerce.

Management of aggregate demand in the economy.

Each of the reasons is discussed briefly below.

Provision of essential services

Governments may provide certain services such as health, education, policing, sanitation, etc. for everyone regardless of their ability to pay. Such services are sometimes referred to as merit goods: governments may regard it as meritorious or morally right to secure equality of access to such goods and services.

Transfer payments

Transfer payments are payments for which no goods or services have been offered in return and are intended usually as a means of maintaining living standards for those in society who are in most need. Examples include unemployment benefits and state pensions.

Natural monopolies

Generally, economists believe that competition is beneficial because it provides consumers with the maximum choice of suppliers and provides maximum incentives for firms to produce efficiently. However, governments may decide to intervene directly in certain sectors of the economy where, for technical reasons, competition cannot occur. For example, governments are likely to intervene where there are large investments in distribution systems so that it is prohibitively expensive to lay down more than one system, such as telecommunications, gas, water and electricity (the public utilities). In post-war UK such natural monopolies have been state-owned: governments, both Labour and Conservative, felt that private ownership of natural monopolies was socially and economically unacceptable. Under Conservative governments since 1979, however, the telecommunications, gas and water industries have been privatized, and the privatization of the electricity industry is planned for the early 1990s. This has diminished the role of the state but has not removed it altogether. The newly privatized public utilities remain state-regulated in terms of their pricing policies and service levels.

Social costs and benefits

Governments intervene to control or prohibit certain goods and services which are considered to have a detrimental effect on society, for example drugs and pornography. In addition, governments may also intervene to protect society from the side-effects of others actions, for instance the control of pollution and the prosecution of polluters. Such side-effects (or spillover effects) are called *social costs* or *external costs*. Equally, governments often promote the supply of goods and services which are considered to have appreciable *social* or *external benefits*, for example the provision of free inoculations against infectious diseases. Government intervention with regard to control of these spillovers may take many forms including laws and regulations, fines and compensation payments, and taxes and subsidies to reduce or stimulate supply.

Support for industry and commerce

Just as governments provide support for individuals, so they may also choose to support firms. This may take the form of industrial and regional aid – notably grants, subsidies and tax concessions. Governments support firms for a variety of reasons – social and political as well as economic. The economic reasons include a desire to increase investment, to finance risky research and development, to redistribute employment, to increase total employment and to benefit exports.

Management of aggregate demand in the economy

Government may intervene to control and stimulate the level of economic activity in the economy. This is based on the view that, left to its own devices, the free market does not necessarily lead to full employment of the nation's scarce resources and therefore operation on its optimum production possibility curve. Equally, the free market might lead to high inflation. Government intervention for much of the post-war period in the UK and elsewhere was directed mainly at regulating the level of aggregate demand in the economy to influence employment and prices. More recently, attention has switched towards stimulating the supply of goods and services in the private sector (*supply-side economics*) and away from *demand management*. Whether governments should aim to control demand, especially through changes in taxation and public spending, is a major theme of this book.

Government economic objectives

Governments have a number of economic objectives, although the importance of each and the trade-offs between them vary from time to time. Several of these have been mentioned already; they are:

1. A high and sustained level of economic growth.
2. Full employment of economic resources, including labour.
3. Low or zero inflation.
4. A sound balance of payments coupled with a strong currency value in the foreign exchange markets.

From time to time other objectives may be emphasized such as a reduction in regional imbalances, a redistribution of income and wealth, more or less state ownership, and promotion of competition and private enterprise. The pursuance of these objectives is made all the more difficult by the existence of policy conflicts or what are often called policy *trade-offs*. Trade-offs may arise, such as between a lower rate of inflation and a higher rate of employment, in the policy measures adopted by government. Subsequent chapters explore many of these policy conflicts.

Economic targets and instruments

In attempting to understand the ways in which governments manage economies, it is important to appreciate the distinction between *policy instruments*, *policy targets* and *policy goals*. The relationship can be summarized as follows:

Targets may be defined as quantifiable aims set by governments and which governments attempt to achieve using policy instruments. Examples of policy targets might be: economic growth in real terms (allowing for inflation) of say 2% per annum; the reduction of unemployment by fifty thousand per annum; restriction of retail price inflation to 4% per annum, and so on. Once the policy targets are set, governments may choose from a range of policy instruments in their efforts to achieve them. Instruments may include changes in the level and structure of interest rates; credit restrictions and other monetary controls; exchange controls; changes in taxation, etc. A policy goal is what the government is ultimately attempting to achieve, e.g. stable prices or full employment. This distinction between policy targets, instruments and goals features in later chapters, especially in the discussion of fiscal and monetary policies in Chapters 5 and 6.

The structure of this book

In this chapter we have provided a foundation for the more detailed and structured analyses of the macroeconomy which follow. In the next chapter we set the scene for the later discussion of economic policies by providing an overview of the performance of the UK economy in recent years, highlighting the record on economic growth, the changing structure of employment, inflation, the balance of payments and exchange rates, as well as changes in the industrial and commercial structure of the economy. Chapter 3 provides a theoretical framework for understanding the inter-relationships within an economy; this framework is referred to as the circular flow of income model and is an essential prerequisite for managers who wish to understand the essence of the economic environment. This is developed further in Chapter 4 which considers the impact of changes in certain macroeconomic variables upon the economy and the determination of the national income.

Chapters 5 to 7 focus on the major policy measures at the disposal of governments in their attempts to manage the economy: Chapter 5 deals with fiscal policy, Chapter 6 with monetary policy and Chapter 7 with supply-side measures. In each of these chapters we attempt to provide the essence of these policies in non-technical language and to identify the reasons and extent to which they have evolved or been displaced in recent years. Chapters 8 and 9 look at the international economy, and more specifically at international trading relationships, the balance of payments and exchange rate systems. These chapters are particularly relevant in the context of the current climate of increasing international economic integration, especially within a European framework, and the globalization of production and trade.

Lastly, Chapter 10 provides seven case studies which draw upon the material in the previous chapters. They are intended to test the reader's understanding of the economic relationships covered in the book and, where appropriate, can form the basis for group or class discussion. Readers will notice that they cover issues discussed regularly in the press and in economic commentaries on television and radio. The purpose of this chapter is to provide an insight into current economic issues which are part of the economic environment in which managers operate.

2

Performance of the economy

The essence of the economy's performance

As Chapter 1 stressed, the performance of the economy has a direct impact upon the success or failure of any firm. Even apparently well managed firms can collapse when Managers ignore or are caught out by changes in the macroeconomic environment. A sound business strategy requires, therefore, an understanding of the current economic situation and some ability to anticipate changes in it. As a backcloth to understanding the current state of the economy and likely trends, however, we need to appreciate the way in which the economy has developed, particularly in recent years.

In this chapter we consider the UK's economic performance in the post-war period. More specifically we look at the country's record on economic growth, productivity and profitability, employment, inflation and the balance of payments and exchange rates. We also discuss underlying changes in the structure of the economy and especially the relative decline in the importance of manufacturing as an economic activity and its displacement by a large, service-based sector.

Economic growth

Economic growth is the term used to describe expansion of the productive capacity of the economy. In practice, the most commonly cited measures are the rate of growth in *gross national product* (GNP) and *gross domestic product* (GDP). Both are measures of the economy's total output (see Chapter 3 for a discussion of national income measures). In terms of the production possibility curve (PPC) introduced in Chapter 1 (Figure 1.2), economic growth involves moving the curve outwards so that more of all goods and services can be produced and hence consumed. Economic growth is, therefore, the source of material wealth. Although economic growth has costs in terms of more pollution, overcrowding and the destruction of the natural environment, over the last two centuries it has been the source of a substantial rise in living standards. It remains to be seen, however, whether this will continue.

The performance of the UK economy in terms of economic growth is central to an appreciation of the other economic problems facing the country (which we review later in this book). In this section we report firstly on the UK's long-term record on economic growth before shedding some light on the Conservative government's claim to have transformed the fortunes of the UK economy in the 1980s.

The UK's long-term record

In the early nineteenth century, the UK became the world's first industrialized economy. Entrepreneurs such as Arkwright in textiles, Bolton, Watt and Stephenson in steam engines, and Brunel in civil engineering (along with countless and now forgotten workers who toiled in the new factories) created an economic wealth previously unknown. By the mid-nineteenth century the UK could justifiably be called 'the workshop of the world'.

Looking back at this period when the UK economy was pre-eminent, we might be excused for thinking that subsequently there has been a serious deterioration in economic performance. Today, only around seven per cent of world trade originates in the UK and few British products now dominate world markets. Moreover, the bulk of world trade is no longer undertaken in vessels built in British shipyards – indeed the British merchant shipbuilding industry has now almost disappeared. A similar picture can be painted for steel production, despite a slight revival in fortunes in the

1980s, textiles and for the coal industry. The coal industry was at the leading edge of the Industrial Revolution but has contracted dramatically in recent years in its effort to reduce government support and attain financial viability.

Not only have the staple industries of the UK economy founded in the nineteenth century declined or disappeared, a number of industries which expanded much more recently and were important in world markets after the Second World War have also shrunk in recent years. For example, the UK motorcycle industry has almost disappeared and, until the arrival of Japanese investment in the 1980s, the UK motor car industry seemed destined to go the same way. Certain parts of the chemical industry have also wound down, especially bulk chemicals and artificial fibres (though other parts, notably pharmaceuticals, have continued to expand). Perhaps most importantly, the mechanical engineering industry, a keystone of the post-war economy, since the late 1970s has undergone painful rationalization and restructuring in the face of competition from more efficient foreign competitors. This is reflected in the figures for the industry's total sales, exports and employment given in Table 2.1. Between 1979 and 1987 sales fell by 21 per cent, exports by 16 per cent and employment by 310,000.

There can be no disputing the fact that the UK is no longer the world's workshop. Instead, the country struggles to maintain a position as a middle ranking industrial nation. Nevertheless, it is important to view the economic changes of the post-war period in a proper historical perspective. Although the UK was the world's primary industrial power in the mid-nineteenth

Table 2.1 Sales, exports and employment in the UK mechanical engineering industry

	Sales[a]	Exports[a]	Employment (000)
1979	124	117	1,022
1980	113	110	997
1981	97	98	879
1982	99	94	852
1983	92	84	777
1984	94	91	758
1985	100	100	756
1986	98	97	730
1987	98	98	712

[a] Index 1985 = 100.
Source: Annual Abstract of Statistics (London: HMSO, 1989).

century, its hold on this position was already under threat. One purpose of the 1851 Great Exhibition in London was to market British manufactured goods facing a threat from new competition from abroad. In 1886, a Royal Commission reported on 'The Depression of Trade and Industry' and this, along with reports from other enquiries, identified as contributory factors poor labour relations, weaknesses in training and education, inadequate investment, poor marketing and the inability of British salesmen to speak foreign languages – all familiar clichés in today's world.

Back in the late nineteenth century the threat to UK industry did not come, as now, from the Far East and Japan (the Japanese were still sending people to the UK to learn from the best of our methods) but from the USA and later from Germany. By 1914, Britain's dominance in manufacuring had already been challenged successfully. The economic costs subsequently imposed by two world wars merely accelerated the process by which the UK was overtaken by other industrializing nations.

It would be wrong, however, to state that the British economy has declined in *absolute* terms. If the economy had been in absolute decline then living standards in the UK would have fallen this century, in fact they have risen spectacularly. This is most obviously reflected in the growth in the ownership of consumer durables such as cars and domestic appliances, improved housing and home ownership, and more leisure time. The data in Table 2.2 confirm that average real incomes per head (i.e. adjusted for price rises) rose almost three-fold between 1900 and 1980 and that the average expenditure per head on major consumer durables increased even faster in the same period.

It is rather the case that the UK has failed to match some of the economic growth rates achieved elsewhere, notably most recently in Japan and West Germany. In other words, there has been a *relative* decline in economic performance as measured by rates of economic growth. Moreover, this failure did not begin recently. Annual rates of growth in total output per decade are shown in Figure 2.1 for the periods 1900–38 and 1950–83 for various countries. Note that while the gap between the rate of economic growth in France, Germany, Italy and Japan (though not the USA) and the UK has widened in the second half of this century, it was already opening up much earlier. The UK's relatively poor growth performance is also confirmed if we study the data for the post-war period alone, as in Table 2.3. For example, between 1960 and 1979 UK production in general expanded by only around two-thirds or less of the rates achieved in other major industrial economies.

Is this relatively slow economic growth due to the growth rate slowing down in the UK since the nineteenth century, or has it simply speeded up elsewhere leaving the UK behind? To shed some light on this, Figure

Table 2.2 Real income per head at constant prices[a] and expenditure per head on selected items

	Income per head	Expenditure on cars and motor cycles	Other consumer durables
	£	£	£
1900	1,249	0.78[b]	37.5[c]
1920	1,267	4.71	24.5
1950	1,888	6.64	42.7
1970	3,003	75.90	71.4
1980[d]	3,555	112.70	125.3

[a] Measured as GDP per head at constant (1980) prices.
[b] Including other non-durable items.
[c] 1900 figure includes cars and motor cycles.
[d] Income per head figure is for 1982.
Source: adapted from T. Liesner, 'Economic statistics 1900–1983' (London: Economist Publications, 1985), tables IV.3 and IV.5.

Source: Liesner, *op. cit.*, chart IV.1.

Figure 2.1 Comparative rates of growth in retail output 1900–38 and 1950–83.

Table 2.3 Comparative rates of growth in the post-war period

	UK	USA	France	W. Germany	Italy	Japan
1950–60	2.66	3.26	4.56	7.97	5.54[a]	8.82
1960–73	2.28	4.17	5.56	4.43	5.30	10.43
1973–83	2.22	2.04	2.23	1.64	1.80	3.70

[a] 1951–60.   *Source:* Liesner, *op. cit.,* table IV.1.

Source: N. F. R. Crafts, S. J. Leybourne and T. C. Mills, 'Trends and cycles in British industrial production, 1700–1913', *Journal of the Royal Statistical Society,* series A (1989), vol. 152, part 1, p. 53.

Figure 2.2 Trend rate of economic growth 1700–1920.

2.2 provides a graph of the UK's economic growth rate from the start of the eighteenth century to 1920. It should be appreciated that the figures, especially for the earlier periods, must be taken as only broad estimates. Nevertheless, what is interesting is the consistency in the UK's performance. In general terms, the UK's trend growth rate hovered between 2 and 3 per cent through much of the nineteenth century, just as it has done since the Second World War. Apparently it is not so much that anything has happened this century to slow down the growth of the British economy, but that emerging industrializing competitors have been able to achieve much faster growth rates than the UK – rates that the UK did not experience even when it was the workshop of the world.

It is difficult to identify precisely why the British economy has failed to achieve the faster economic growth experienced elsewhere, especially in the boom years for world trade in the 1950s and 1960s. Economists have identified a number of possible economic and social reasons – most are reminiscent of those identified in the official reports of the late nineteenth century referred to earlier, namely poor education and training, weak labour relations, slow population growth, low investment, low profitability, the social structure (a class-based society), an overdependence on slow growing markets of the former British Empire and excessive state intervention. No consensus, however, exists among economists as to which of these causes is the most important. The UK's poor performance relative to other major economies appears to be the product of a number of interrelated economic and social weaknesses.

Recent performance of the UK economy

In the 1980s, the Conservative government introduced a number of economic and social reforms aimed at improving Britain's economic performance (discussed in detail in Chapter 7). Some economists have claimed that, consequently, there has been a sharp improvement in Britain's relative economic growth rate (the so-called Thatcher miracle). But others have argued that it is still too soon to claim that the trend rate of growth has improved.

In interpreting the economic record of the 1980s, the choice of an appropriate base date for comparative purposes is critical. The economy suffered a severe recession between 1979 and 1981 when real GDP fell by 1.8% (the only example of an absolute economic decline in the post-war period). Therefore, taking 1980 or 1981 as the base date for comparison with later years would exaggerate the scale of the subsequent economic recovery. In contrast, taking 1978 or 1979 as the starting point reduces the average growth rate in later years. The increase in real GDP averaged + 1.8% per annum between 1979 and 1988 but nearly twice that rate, + 3.4% per annum, if the period 1982 to 1988 is selected. Therefore, while the economic growth record based upon the period 1979–88 does not support the idea of a 'Thatcher miracle', the growth rate for 1982–8 gives more cause for optimism – although even this growth is not much faster than that achieved in the 1960s.

The 1980s was a more difficult period for the world economy in general than the 1960s. Therefore, a more reliable indicator of the UK's economic performance might be obtained by comparing the UK's economic growth rate with that of our main competitors in the 1980s. The result of this comparison is presented in Figure 2.3. Here the UK's growth rate is expressed as a percentage of the average growth rate of the other major economies (those affiliated under the umbrella of the Organization for Economic Co-operation and Development – OECD). Taking a base date

UK GDP growth as a percentage of OECD growth

Source: D. McWilliams, 'The Renaissance of British Management', *Business Studies* November 1989, p. 20.

Figure 2.3 UK economic growth – international comparisons.

of 1980 (a compromise between 1979 and 1982), it appears that not only did the UK improve its performance in the 1980s, but it also grew slightly faster than the economies of the OECD as a whole. The chart also highlights the disappointing rate of growth of the UK economy in the 1970s. It seems that the UK achieved a much improved comparative performance in the 1980s, especially compared with our relative performance in the immediately preceding decade.

What is unclear at the start of the 1990s, however, is whether the economic recovery experienced in the 1980s is simply a catching-up exercise, reflecting the low growth of the 1970s, or whether the UK economy has managed to break away from its earlier long-term growth rate as reflected in Figures 2.2 and 2.3. In 1989, the government increased interest rates to record levels (relative to inflation) in an attempt to reduce growth in the economy in the face of rising inflation and a substantial balance of payments deficit. The government has claimed that this action amounted to a temporary slowing down of economic growth following a slight 'overheating' of the economy. Critics, however, have claimed that the 1980s was the exceptional period and that the fast economic growth experienced then has once again proved unsustainable. Previous fast periods of growth (though over a shorter period than in the 1980s), for example in 1972–3, also ended in rising inflation and a balance of payments crisis.

Productivity and profitability

Just as there is uncertainty about how far the trend rate of economic growth in the UK has risen, so it is unclear to what extent the economy has permanently improved its record on productivity. Productivity and economic growth are closely related. High economic growth requires success in solving the 'economic problem' discussed in the previous chapter. In other words, scarce economic resources must be used efficiently. One indicator of the efficient use of resources is productivity, which expresses outputs in terms of the inputs of factors of production needed to produce the outputs. Outputs can be expressed relative to labour inputs only (numbers employed or the total number of hours worked in a given period) and the result is called labour productivity or *partial factor productivity*. Alternatively, productivity can be measured taking into account non-labour as well as labour inputs, notably capital equipment, to provide a *total factor productivity* series.

Table 2.4 sets out the UK record on labour productivity compared with that of our major competitors. Once again, while labour productivity rose in the UK, it increased generally at a slower rate than in most other countries until 1979. Since 1980, however, the economy's labour productivity performance has been good both in historical terms and compared with the rates achieved in other major economies. The estimates of total factor (land, labour and capital) productivity growth in Figure 2.4 confirm the improvement in performance from the late 1970s, though given the difficulty in accurately measuring capital inputs these figures must be treated as rough approximations only. At the same time, it should be appreciated that an improvement in labour productivity, brought about largely as a result of shedding surplus labour, can take some time to feed through into higher total output.

As in the case of economic growth, however, controversy surrounds whether the productivity improvement in the 1980s amounts to a permanent increase in the trend rate of productivity growth or whether it is simply a reflection of the productivity growth experienced in the 1970s. For much of the 1970s productivity growth (both labour and total factor productivity) was negligible, implying considerable scope for raising productivity in the UK.

The relatively poor performance in terms of productivity up to the 1980s was reflected in business profits. A low growth in productivity means that wage demands cannot be met without raising costs. At the

Table 2.4 Labour productivity growth –
international comparisons

	Output per person employed		
	1960–70	1970–80	1980–8
Whole economy			
UK	2.4	1.3	2.5
USA	2.0	0.4	1.2
Japan	8.9	3.8	2.9
W. Germany	4.4	2.8	1.8
France	4.6	2.8	2.0
Italy	6.3	2.6	2.0
Canada	2.4	1.5	1.4
Average	3.5	1.7	1.8
Manufacturing industry only			
UK	3.0	1.6	5.2
USA	3.5	3.0	4.0
Japan	8.8	5.3	3.1
W. Germany	4.1	2.9	2.2
France	5.4	3.2	3.1
Italy	5.4	3.0	3.5
Canada	3.4	3.0	3.6
Average	4.5	3.3	3.6

Source: H.M. Treasury, *Economic Progress
Report,* no. 201 (April 1989), p. 1.

Source: T. Venables, 'Productivity change in the UK', *Economic Review*
(September, 1989), table 2, p. 36.

Figure 2.4 UK total factor productivity growth.

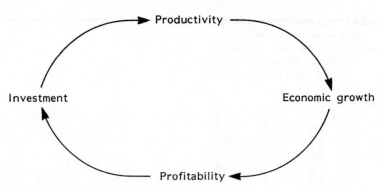

Figure 2.5 The growth cycle.

same time, a slowly expanding home market provides a weak base for increasing sales revenue. The rate of return on capital for much of the post-war period has been lower in the UK than in the economies of our major competitors. For example, between 1974 and 1979, rates of return in the business sector averaged 19.7 per cent in the USA, 21.6 per cent in Japan, 16.3 per cent in West Germany, 16.1 per cent in France and 20.9 per cent in Italy, but only 11.7 per cent in the UK. In addition, profitability declined sharply in the 1970s as economic growth and productivity stagnated.

In contrast, an outstanding feature of the UK economy in the 1980s has been the recovery in business profitability, although rates of return on investment still remain lower than in competitor economies. High profits tend to be associated with high investment since there are more retained earnings to invest and investment is profitable. At the same time, high investment promotes a further rise in productivity which spills over into faster economic growth. The recent recovery in business profitability, therefore, provides a basis for greater optimism about the likely path of the UK's economic performance in the 1990s than existed in the 1970s. In the 1970s the economy appeared to be locked into a low productivity– low growth–low profitability–low investment cycle, as illustrated by Figure 2.5.

Employment

High economic growth depends upon the efficient use of economic resources. Unemployment of labour and capital involves a waste of

Source: Department of Employment, *Employment Gazette* (February 1990).
Figure 2.6 Total unemployment in the UK.

economic resources. Nevertheless, whether by design or neglect, unemployment in the UK during the early 1980s grew to a level not seen since the 1930s. In the early 1980s, unemployment of labour rose to well over three million (Figure 2.6) and capacity utilization in industry (a measure of the employment of capital equipment) declined sharply. After the Second World War and up until the early 1970s it had been a major policy objective of successive governments in the UK – both Conservative and Labour – to maintain 'full' employment, interpreted as an unemployment rate of around 2 to 3 per cent. Some unemployment always exists in economies reflecting temporary registration when people change jobs, regional imbalances in the level of economic activity, structural changes within the economy and an inability or unwillingness by some people to accept the jobs on offer. Therefore, some economists now argue that by attempting to maintain such a low unemployment rate through public expenditure programmes, governments encouraged inflation during this period. An overly tight labour market drove up wages as employers competed for the labour available, at the same time increasing the bargaining power of trade unions.

No economic subject is more emotive and controversial than unemployment. Economists argue over what is the optimal unemployment rate that will maximize economic growth without spilling over into inflation. Politicians, whose task it is to chose and implement economic policy, worry also about what rate of unemployment is socially and politically acceptable. Particularly controversial is the notion of a so-called *natural rate of unemployment*, a phrase associated with free market economists.

The natural rate of unemployment is defined as that rate of unemployment which exists when the demand for labour equals the supply of labour
that is willing to work at the wage rates on offer. These wage rates are the
real (inflation-adjusted) wage rates and reflect the real cost for businesses
of employing labour. Other things being equal, when real wages rise the
cost of employing labour increases and so fewer people are employed.
Similarly, if the real wage falls, industry will demand more labour and so
more people are employed. The natural rate of unemployment is therefore
that rate of unemployment which an economy can expect to achieve
without triggering inflationary pressures in the labour market. It should
be noted that this rate implies some continuing unemployment in addition
to the 'inevitable' unemployment noted above, since not everyone
may be willing to work at the going real wage.

The natural rate of unemployment is, therefore, associated with a
particular level of *voluntary* unemployment at any particular time, reflecting
the relative benefits of working and not working. It is important to note
that those unemployed are not necessarily social welfare scroungers or
dole cheats: they have simply made a rational economic choice not to
work given the current wages on offer (relative to the cost of living) and
their preference for leisure over work. In so far as state welfare benefits
make it easier to turn down low-waged jobs, however, some economists
believe that a generous welfare state system raises the level of unemployment. When welfare benefits rise in real terms, the relative costs and
benefits of working or not working change. More people can be expected to
reject low paid jobs: they decide that they are 'better off' on the dole.

Not all economists are happy with the concept of a natural rate of
unemployment. In addition others, while accepting the general idea, find
difficulty in applying it. What is the market-clearing real wage at present?
Can we estimate it? Does it always follow that the rate of unemployment
is responsive to changes in state welfare payments? Even if it is, is cutting
welfare benefits a socially or morally acceptable way of reducing unemployment? Are there better ways? These are but a few of the questions that
arise in trying to address this issue.

In the 1980s, government economic policy was influenced by the idea
of a natural unemployment rate in broadly two ways:

1. Economic policy was concerned with reducing unemployment to the
   natural rate and not to the low rates of full employment found in the
   1950s and 1960s: i.e. higher rates of unemployment were tolerated to
   keep down inflation.

2. The government believed that the only way to reduce unemployment
   in the longer term and without triggering higher inflation was to

reduce the underlying natural rate of unemployment: i.e. unemployment was best tackled by changing the relative costs and benefits of working or not working, rather than by manipulating the level of aggregate demand for goods and services in the economy.

The consequent shift in government economic policy on unemployment, away from *aggregate demand management* policies towards *supply-side* policies, has proved to be the most dramatic economic policy change of the 1980s (see Chapter 7 for details).

In addition to the rise in unemployment in recent years, other noteworthy developments affecting the labour market have been the change in the distribution of labour between manufacturing and service industries and the decline in trade union membership. There is a growing economic problem on the horizon, however, arising from changes in demographics and the age composition of the labour force.

The changing distribution of labour

The fall in employment in the UK's manufacturing sector is illustrated in Table 2.5 and mirrors the relative uncompetitiveness of UK manufacturing in world markets. As market shares in motor manufacturing, textiles, steel, shipbuilding, consumer electronics and many areas of engineering have declined, so lay-offs have occurred. There was an especially marked fall in employment in manufacturing in the early 1980s when the competitiveness of UK industry was further undermined by both a high exchange rate and high interest rates. At the same time, however, there has been a substantial growth in service sector employment, notably in retailing, public admini-

Table 2.5 Changes in the distribution of UK employment 1950-88

		Percentage employment in:		
	Agriculture	Manufac-turing	Distribu-tion[a] and service	Other
1950	3	37	31	29
1960	3	35	35	27
1970	2	34	40	24
1980	1	27	48	24
1988	1	23	53	23

[a] Excludes transport and communication but includes public administration.
Source: Derived from Liesner, *op. cit.*, table IV.6, and 1988 figure from *Social Trends* (London: HMSO, 1989), table 4.10.

stration, teaching, banking and insurance and other office work. In part, this shift in the structure of employment in the economy reflects a general movement experienced in all 'mature' industrial economies towards replacing people by machines in manufacturing and towards more employment in the distribution and services sectors. As real incomes rise, so people tend to spend more on services such as insurance, travel and retailing. Moreover, distribution and service sector jobs have so far been less easy to mechanize than those in industry, although this is now quickly changing with the onset of computerization in the financial services and retailing sectors.

Decline in trade union membership

Trade union membership rose throughout the post-war period in Britain to a peak of just over 13 million members, covering approximately 50 per cent of the workforce, by 1979. Much of this growth, however, was located in manufacturing and the public services. In the public sector, around 80 per cent of employees were in unions by 1979 compared with around 40 per cent of workers in the private sector. In general, unionization remained especially low in private service industries. Therefore, the onset of the sharp decline in manufacturing employment in the early 1980s, alongside tight restraints upon public spending, caused union membership to fall sharply to 10.5 million by 1986 (around 40 per cent of the total workforce).

The decline in trade union membership has been matched by a decline in the economic power of trade unions. This decline in power was partly a consequence of high unemployment and partly the result of trade union legislation passed by the Conservative government in the 1980s. The Employment Acts, 1980, 1982, 1988 and 1989, along with the Trades Union Act, 1984, significantly reduced the freedom of trade unions to call strikes without prior strike ballots and to picket, especially away from the strikers' own workplaces (for more details of this legislation see Chapter 7). A further piece of legislation aimed at restricting unofficial or 'wildcat' strikes will be on the statute books in 1990. This legislation plus rising unemployment was associated with a sharp fall in the number of days lost in industry through industrial disputes during the first half of the 1980s (excluding 1984 where the figure was inflated by the long coal miners' dispute – see Figure 2.7). Like the trends in economic growth and productivity reviewed earlier, however, the recent record on strikes must be interpreted with caution. Some economists question whether there has been a fundamental change in attitudes in British labour relations which will guarantee less labour militancy if full employment returns. The number of working days lost through stoppages began to rise again as unemployment fell after 1986.

Source: Department of Employment, *Employment Gazette* (February 1990).

Figure 2.7 Working days lost in the UK through industrial disputes (all industries and services).

Table 2.6 Demographic changes in the UK

	Percentage of population in different age groups		
	Under 15	15–64	64+
1950	22.3	67.0	10.7
1980	21.1	64.0	14.9
1991ª	19.1	65.0	15.9
2001ª	20.3	64.1	15.6
2011ª	18.5	65.3	16.2

ª Forecast.
Source: Liesner, *op. cit.*, table IV.9; projections from *Social Trends* (London: HMSO, 1989), table 1.2.

Demographic changes

As the threat of strikes has receded, many managers in the UK have become more concerned about current changes in the demographic structure of the labour force as set out in Table 2.6. In the early 1980s the number of 16 to 21 year olds entering the labour market rose because of the post-war 'baby boom'. In the 1970s, however, the birth rate declined sharply. Consequently, there will be a major shortfall in the numbers of young people available to firms in the 1990s.

As the number of 16 to 21 year olds falls, so the average age of the population rises. Therefore, with fewer young people and more people over the age of 40, firms will increasingly have to turn to employing older workers and more females, especially mothers wishing to return to work. In addition, workers will need to participate in retraining on a more frequent basis, as the needs of the labour market alter. Fewer workers can look forward with confidence to a 'lifetime' career with the same employer or even in the same line of work. One estimate suggests that in the future people will, on average, have to make a major change in their employment at least three times during their working lives. These developments, which to a large extent reflect trends in other western countries, have obvious implications for the provision of education and training in the UK.

The aging of the labour force will also be reflected in a greater proportion of people of retirement age in the population. Continuing improvements in health care mean that people are living longer while retiring earlier. Consequently, the non-employed population has to be supported by a smaller number of employed. This prospect led the Conservative government in 1986 to amend the state earnings-related pension scheme (known as SERPS) to reduce the future economic burden on taxpayers. It is also leading firms to review their marketing plans and product lines. An aging population has relevance especially to consumer goods industries and services such as retailing. In general, the elderly do not buy clothes from boutiques. They also tend to take a different type of holiday and stay in a different type of hotel. Their housing needs are very different from those of the younger generations, with implications for developments such as retirement homes and sheltered housing. They may even look for different qualities in a motor car – safety over acceleration for instance. The changing age structure of the population imposes an important economic challenge to managers in the 1990s.

Inflation

Whereas prices fell in the depression years of the inter-war period, in the post-war era prices have risen. Inflation only became a major economic problem, however, in the 1970s. Prior to this period the economy suffered from 'creeping inflation' of around 5 per cent. This low rate did not impose a major threat to the economy; indeed a low rate of inflation can be economically beneficial since firms buy in raw materials and components which appreciate in value. Also, low inflation means that international competitiveness declines only slowly. Nevertheless, in the 1960s and early 1970s governments felt a need to introduce specific measures, e.g. prices and incomes policies, to try and reduce inflationary pressures.

Source: Department of Employment, *Employment Gazette* (February 1990).

Figure 2.8 UK retail price inflation.

With the onset of the oil crisis of 1973–4, inflation accelerated significantly, peaking at over 25 per cent in 1975. Subsequently, it declined until 1978 when a combination of pressures caused it to rise again. These included a further jump in world oil prices and a change in the rate of value added tax (VAT) from 8 to 15 per cent in 1979, along with higher wage settlements during and after the 1978–9 'winter of discontent', when labour strikes threatened to bring the country to a standstill. Inflation reached 18 per cent in 1980 before tighter monetary policy began to bring the rate down (the principles and practice of monetary policy are discussed in Chapter 6). By 1986 inflation had fallen to under 4 per cent; in other words back to around the creeping rate of the 1960s. Subsequently, it began to rise again as the economy expanded and unemployment fell. By the end of 1989 it had reached almost 8 per cent (refer to Figure 2.8).

In general, the UK's inflation rate has been disappointing compared with the record of many of our competitors. Table 2.7 compares average rates of inflation in the UK against average rates in a number of other major economies. What is apparent is the way that the UK's performance mirrors international fluctuations in inflation, but with the UK generally performing worse than its major competitors, especially West Germany. Even in the mid-1980s, the UK's rate of inflation, compared with West Germany,

Table 2.7 Comparative inflation rates

	UK	USA	France	W. Ger- many	Italy	Japan
1950–60	4.11	2.09	5.89	1.76	2.94	4.03
1960–73	5.05	3.18	4.20	3.41	4.71	5.58
1973–83	13.60	8.37	11.28	4.73	16.97	8.39

Source: Liesner, *op. cit.*, table IV.10.

remained unsatisfactory. Moreover, in the 1960s and 1970s and again from the mid-1980s onwards a rise in the level of UK economic activity and falling unemployment tended to be associated with a rise in the inflation rate. Successive UK governments since the early 1960s have wrestled without much success with the problem of how to marry a high level of economic activity and a low rate of inflation.

The balance of payments and the exchange rate

The effect of inflation on the international competitiveness of British industry is reflected in the balance of payments and the exchange rate for sterling against other leading currencies. Immediately after the war, sterling was valued at its pre-war level against the US dollar of £1 = $4.03, but this proved unsustainable. Sterling was devalued in September 1949 to £1 = £2.80 and remained at this value for almost two decades. During the 1950s and 1960s most countries, including the UK, kept their exchange rates fixed against one another in accordance with an international agreement entered into at Bretton Woods, New Hampshire in 1944 (for a fuller discussion of this agreement and post-war exchange rate policy, see Chapter 9). Most balance of payments problems were tackled through deflationary fiscal and monetary policies (whereby governments attempted to reduce demand in the economy and hence the demand for foreign goods) rather than by devaluation. During the mid-1960s, however, the confidence of international investors in sterling declined, leading to the sterling crisis of November 1967 when the Labour government reluctantly devalued the currency, this time to £1 = $2.40.

The post-war system of fixed exchange rates came to an end in the mid-1970s. Rising world inflation spurred on by the oil price hike of 1973–4 led most countries to abandon fixed rates. Currencies were *floated*

1980 = 100

Source: Financial Statistics (London: HMSO).

Figure 2.9 UK exchange rate index 1979–89.

and allowed to find their own market levels. Sterling was allowed to float from June 1972 and since then, taking the long-term trend, has depreciated, especially against a trade-weighted index of other leading currencies (see Figure 2.9). This reflects the UK's high inflation rate compared with other major trading countries. But around this trend there have been sharp fluctuations: in particular, sterling rose in value by over 20 per cent between the start of 1979 and the end of 1980 because of a combination of high interest rates in the UK and the beneficial impact on the balance of payments of North Sea oil production. This rise in the value of sterling at a time of high inflation caused a sharp loss of competitiveness in foreign trade leading to the severe fall in manufacturing output and employment referred to earlier.

The balance of payments is discussed in detail in Chapter 8. Briefly, it is made up of the *balance of trade* in goods, net earnings from the sale of services abroad (which added to the balance of trade gives what is called the *current balance*) and capital imports and exports (movements in holdings of *external* assets and liabilities). Figure 2.10 presents summary data on the current balance between 1979 and 1989. What is immediately apparent is the major improvement that took place in this balance in the early 1980s, despite the uncompetitiveness of UK manufacturing. This improvement resulted from the economic recession at that time, which held down the

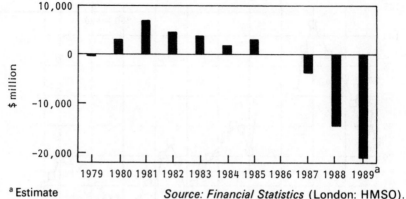

ᵃ Estimate   *Source: Financial Statistics* (London: HMSO).

Figure 2.10 UK current account balance 1979–89.

expansion of imports, and from the benefits from North Sea oil in terms of direct export earnings and as a substitute for previously imported oil.

After 1982, however, the surplus on the current account began to decline. The deterioration accelerated from 1986 as world oil prices collapsed from over $30 a barrel to around $10 by 1988, sharply reducing the revenue from oil exports. Also, as the economy recovered, there was an increase in domestic expenditure on imported consumer and investment goods. By the end of 1989 the UK was running a forecast annual balance of payments deficit on current account of £20bn. It was this mounting deficit combined with rising inflation which led the UK government to tighten monetary policy by raising interest rates. Bank base rates, for example, rose from 7.5 per cent in May 1988 to 15 per cent in October 1989.

Concluding remarks

Economies and economic policy do not exist in a historical vacuum. What is happening today in the macroeconomy cannot be fully appreciated without an understanding of past economic trends. In this chapter we have set the scene for discussion of the economic principles and policies presented in the rest of this book. In particular, we have seen that the UK economy has a long record of relatively low economic growth and, since the 1960s, has suffered from relatively high inflation and periodic balance of payments crises. Consequently, macroeconomic policy in the UK has been dominated by the search for a solution to these weaknesses, especially inflation. Many economists believe that until inflation is solved sustainable economic growth, comparable to that experienced by our competitors, will remain impossible. Economic growth will necessarily grind to a halt in the face of rising prices and balance of payments deficits.

Equally, some economists argue that until inflation is brought down permanently unemployment must remain high. In particular, one of the most important controversies in macroeconomics concerns the legitimate role of government in tackling unemployment. Economists divide between those who recommend government action to boost demand in the economy when unemployment is rising (so-called Keynesian economists) and those who favour government action to remove barriers to the operation of competitive markets and to restore stable prices (so-called supply-side economists and monetarists). The next chapter presents a diagrammatic model of the macroeconomy as a basis for exploring this controversy in later chapters.

3

Understanding economic flows

The essence of economic flows

As stressed in Chapter 1, managers need to understand the interrelationships within an economy if they are to appreciate the nature of the macro-economic environment and its impact upon business. Economies are made up of a multitude of economic agents, performing varied roles within the economy both in terms of the production of goods and services and their consumption. Within the economy as a whole, economic agents may be aggregated into one of five broad groups or sectors:

1. The household sector.
2. The firm sector.
3. The government sector.
4. The financial services sector.
5. The foreign sector.

In the study of economies, these sectors and their roles are usually described as follows.

The household sector
At the most basic level, households provide the resources (factors of production) that firms need to produce goods and services. These resources

take the form of labour, land and capital (both physical and financial). In return, households receive from firms payment for these factor services in the form of wages and salaries, rents and interest, profits and dividends. At the same time, these 'incomes' generate expenditure on the goods and services produced by firms: this is referred to as consumer spending or simply as consumption.

The firm sector
In contrast to the household sector, firms employ and reward the factors of production provided by households. The employment of these resources gives rise to the many different types of goods and services produced in an economy which are then bought by households, the government, other firms and foreigners. Firms also perform a vital role in the economy in the form of investment in new plant and machinery, land and buildings and other productive capacity.

The government sector
Governments perform a number of functions within economies. Like firms they are providers of certain goods and services (for example education, health, defence and law and order) and they pay wages to their employees who form part of the household sector. They also purchase the final goods and services of firms thereby adding to total consumption expenditure, and carry out investment through the building of new roads, hospitals, schools, etc. Lastly, governments collect taxes from individuals and companies to finance their expenditure, including making payments (known as 'transfer payments') out of taxation to the unemployed, pensioners, students, the sick and so on.

The financial services sector
This sector of the economy comprises the full range of financial intermediaries – banks, building societies, insurance companies, pension funds, etc. These institutions do not produce any physical (tangible) output and therefore they are usually grouped separately from other firms. They play a vital role in the economy by providing services which channel money from savers to borrowers. Savers are households, firms with surplus funds, foreigners and sometimes public bodies. Likewise borrowers can be all of these.

The foreign sector
Foreigners make a direct contribution to the economy by buying exports and selling imports. Moreover, with an increasingly interdependent world, the importance of foreign capital flows into and out of economies is

growing. These capital flows play an important role alongside domestic savings in financing investment and consumer spending in economies.

Macroeconomics involves the study of the interrelationship between these five sectors and the determination of economic activity by these sectors. Inevitably, aggregation of the activities of economic agents in this way conceals information about individual behaviour. For example, a rise in the economy's total output or income tells us nothing about who receives that output or who earns the incomes. Sometimes in economic analysis it is useful to disaggregate and consider individual decision making: for instance, the individual firm's competitive strategy. In this chapter, however, we are concerned only with understanding the nature of the broad economic flows in economies. Therefore, we can make useful progress by referring to the five broad sectors above. The purpose of this chapter is to present the essence of macroeconomic activity through a simplified version of how actual economies function. The remainder of this chapter is structured as follows:

1. The measurement of economic activity, i.e. *national income accounting.*
2. Problems in calculating economic activity.
3. Compilation and uses of national income accounts.
4. A model of national income determination.

The measurement of economic activity

The interrelationships between the above five sectors of the economy can be summarized diagrammatically as in Figure 3.1. This diagram illustrates the flow of income and spending in an economy and is commonly referred to as the *circular flow of income model.* Although much simplified (for example, all profits are assumed to be distributed to households with none retained by firms; all taxes are imposed upon households) it does capture the essence of the macroeconomy.

The circular flow of income model represents the movement of income between households and firms and also shows the effects of the government, the foreign and the financial sectors on this flow. It will be seen that in the case of the household sector, the extent to which the sum of households' incomes flows back to the firm sector in the form of expenditure is affected by three *leakages* – the amount saved, taxation paid to the government

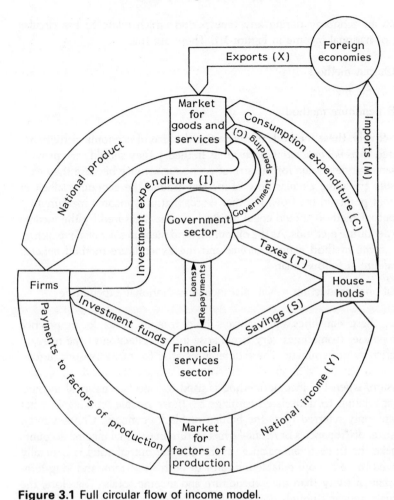

Figure 3.1 Full circular flow of income model.

and the amount spent on imports. At the same time, there are three *injections* into the circular flow taking place, offsetting to some extent the effect of these leakages. These injections are expenditure by government on goods and services, investment expenditure by firms, and receipts from foreigners making payments for our exports. The importance of these flows in the form of leakages and injections in the determination of economic activity is discussed on pages 49–55. Changes in these flows give rise to economic fluctuations. Moreover, attempts by government to influence the flows lie at the heart of macroeconomic management discussed in later chapters.

There are three methods of calculating the size of economic activity within an economy during any time period which relate to the circular flow of national income in Figure 3.1. These are the:

1. Output method.
2. Income method.
3. Expenditure method.

Collectively, these methods of measuring the size of economic activity are referred to as *national income accounting*. In theory they should each provide the same money value for the size of economic activity because they each measure the same circular flow of income around the economy, albeit at different points in the flow. In other words, national income measured by the output method should equal national income measured by the income or expenditure methods. As the output method measures *national production,* the income method *national income* and the expenditure method *national expenditure,* it follows that:

National production = National income = National expenditure

While these equalities must always hold true in principle, in practice discrepancies (sometimes very large) arise in the collection of the relevant statistics by government. These differences arise for many reasons: errors, omissions, timing differences and so on. Perhaps the most significant omission, when the income method is used to calculate national income, is that relating to undeclared earnings by those people working in what is commonly referred to as the hidden or black economy. Consequently, statistical discrepancies or *residual errors* feature in national income accounts to make the three totals balance. In the UK the output total is generally believed to be a more reliable indicator of both short-term and long-term economic activity than the expenditure and income totals. Therefore, the residuals appear (though not always) in the other two totals, reflecting unmeasured expenditure and unmeasured income. In 1988 the residual error attributed to the expenditure method by government statisticians was slightly over £2bn and to the income method £181m. These residual errors would not exist in a world of perfect statistics. Alternatively an *average* of all three totals is often used as the appropriate indicator.

The output method

The output method calculates the total value of the final output of goods and services produced in the economy over a specified period of time. It is important to note that all final goods and services must be included regardless of whether they are sold to consumers, government, foreigners or to other firms in the form of capital equipment. To avoid the problem of *double counting*, and hence overestimation of the country's total output, intermediate production of goods must not be included in the final total. Alternatively, the problem of double counting can be avoided by only summing the *value added* by each firm at the different stages of production, rather than final outputs.

The income method

Since national income arises from the production of goods and services by the factors of production, another way of calculating the value of total output is to sum all of the incomes that these factors receive for their services – wages and salaries, rent, interest, profits and dividends. This method is referred to as the *income method* of measuring the level of economic activity in any time period. It is important to note that only incomes that have been received in return for productive services should be included. Transfer payments, therefore, must be excluded since they merely represent a redistribution of income, for instance from taxpayers to pensioners. Including these payments would lead to double counting and therefore overestimation of national income. In other words, if transfer payments were not excluded, raising pensions, unemployment benefits or similar welfare payments would lead to a statistical increase in national income when the actual output of the economy had not changed.

The expenditure method

By adding up all the money values of expenditures on final goods and services produced in an economy, we arrive at the measurement of *national expenditure*. It should be noted that this will only be equal to national output if we allow for net changes in stocks (inventories) and work in progress. These are normally included in the expenditure total as part of firms' own investment spending. Therefore, national expenditure is the sum of consumption of domestically produced goods, investment expenditure (including an allowance for changes in stocks and work in progress), expenditure by government and net receipts from foreign trade. As before, to avoid double counting, only expenditure on final goods and services should be included.

Problems in calculating economic activity

A number of problems arise when calculating the economy's total flow of national income using the above three methods. These involve:

1. Allowance for capital depreciation and stock appreciation.
2. Valuation of output at market prices or factor (i.e. production) cost.
3. The inclusion of net property income from abroad.

Capital depreciation and stock appreciation

During any given period some investment expenditure will merely be replacing capital, both equipment and buildings, that has worn out during the production of income and output in that period. Therefore, some allowance should be made for depreciation or capital consumption when calculating national income since this investment expenditure does not represent an increase in the economy's productive capacity or wealth. Only *net* investment (after depreciation) represents the true increase in the country's capital stock during the period. Where no allowance is made for depreciation the resulting totals are referred to as *gross* output, income or expenditure; when depreciation is deducted from the gross sum we arrive at the corresponding net figures. We can therefore define the following terms:

Gross national product (GNP) ⎫
Gross national expenditure (GNE) ⎬ − Depreciation
Gross national income (GNI) ⎭

= ⎧ Net national product (NNP)
  ⎨ Net national expenditure (NNE)
  ⎩ Net national income (NNI)

Estimates of depreciation are available for adjusting national income figures from gross to net. Nevertheless, when discussing national income it is common to use the gross rather than the net amounts even though the latter provide a more accurate reflection of the growth in national well-being. This is done for two reasons: because depreciation tends to change relatively slowly over time and hence gross and net figures move closely together; and because it is difficult to make an accurate estimate of depreciation at the national level. In other words, the gross figures are usually more accurate than the net figures.

Just as the government statisticians take account of depreciation or capital consumption when calculating national income figures, so they also adjust their estimates to take account of stock appreciation. It is conventional to subtract from national income totals any increase in the value of the net change in stocks of unsold goods arising from a general increase in prices. The reasoning is similar to that which lies behind adjusting for depreciation. Stock appreciation does not represent a *real* increase in a nation's output. When stock appreciation occurs it is not physical output that grows, as reflected in higher stocks in the economy, it is merely that the stocks have a higher monetary value reflecting a general rise in prices, i.e. inflation.

Market prices and factor cost

National expenditure as described above is measured initially on the basis of market, (i.e. retail) prices – prices paid across the counter. These prices, however, may be distorted by the inclusion of indirect taxes and subsidies. Indirect taxes, such as VAT and excise duties, increase the prices of goods and services, while subsidies have the opposite effect. At the same time, however, national income and national product are both measured at factor cost, that is with respect to the amounts paid to factors of production for their services excluding indirect taxes and subsidies. In order to ensure equivalence across the three methods of measuring national income, market prices must be converted to factor cost by subtracting indirect taxes and adding subsidies. Therefore we can write:

National expenditure
at factor cost   = National expenditure at market prices
                          − Indirect taxes + Subsidies

It is conventional to measure national output at factor cost rather than at market prices, otherwise any changes in indirect taxes or subsidies would distort the estimate of total output irrespective of whether there was a change in the quantity of goods and services produced.

Net property income from abroad

Part of an economy's measured output may have been produced by foreign-owned firms. Likewise, some domestically-owned firms may be producing output abroad. Whether we should allow for all the income resulting from these activities depends upon the purpose for which we are calculating national income. Do we wish to measure only domestic output (literally produced within the country), or do we wish to measure the output of the economy's factors of production wherever they are located? In the former case we arrive at measurements of domestic output, domestic income and domestic expenditure. In the latter case, we can allow for *net property income from abroad*. This represents the difference between the income received by the domestic economy from the production of its firms located overseas minus that income paid to overseas residents from their production in the domestic economy. For instance, profits earned by ICI abroad and remitted to the UK would be included to arrive at national production and income. Similarly, any profits earned by Nissan from producing cars in the UK and remitted to Japan would be excluded. Therefore we can write:

$$\left.\begin{array}{l}\text{Domestic product}\\\text{Domestic income}\\\text{Domestic expenditure}\end{array}\right\} \begin{array}{c}\text{Net property}\\\text{+ income from} =\\\text{abroad}\end{array} \left\{\begin{array}{l}\text{National product}\\\text{National income}\\\text{National expenditure}\end{array}\right.$$

Table 3.1 shows a summarized breakdown of the UK's national income accounts for 1988. Note the distinction between net and gross figures, figures at market prices and factor cost, adjustments for indirect taxes and subsidies, and the effect of net property income from abroad. Also, note the existence of the statistical discrepancy (residual error) term in the calculations using the income and expenditure methods as referred to earlier.

Compilation and uses of national income accounts

In the UK the necessary data to compile the national income accounts, using the above three methods, are collected by government departments and analyzed by government statisticians in the Central Statistical Office (CSO). The main sources of information used for the output method are

Table 3.1 UK national income 1988

	£m current prices	
Output – expenditure method		
Consumer's expenditure		293,569
General government spending on goods and services		91,847
Gross investment		88,751
Value of physical increase in stocks and work in progress		4,371
Exports of goods and services	108,533	
less Imports of goods and services	−125,194	−16,661
Gross domestic product at market prices (expenditure based)		461,877
Statistical discrepancy (residual error)		2,056
Net property income from abroad		5,619
Gross national product at market prices		469,552
less Taxes on expenditure	−75,029	
plus subsidies	5,883	−69,146
Gross national product at factor cost		400,406
less Capital consumption (depreciation)		−54,769
Net national product at factor cost		345,637
Income		
Income from employment		249,775
Income from self-employment		42,617
Gross trading profits of companies		70,242
Gross trading surplus of public corporations		7,286
Gross trading surplus of general government enterprises		−70
Rent		27,464
Other		3,408
less Stock appreciation		−6,116
		394,606
Statistical discrepancy (residual error)		181
Gross domestic product at factor cost (income based)		394,787
Net property income from abroad		5,619
Gross national product at factor cost		400,406
less Capital consumption		−54,769
Net national product at factor cost		345,637

Source: CSO, *United Kingdom National Accounts* (London: HMSO, 1989).

the annual Census of Production and surveys by individual government departments. The income method relies largely upon information from Inland Revenue tax data together with the accounts of central and local government and public corporations. Lastly, the expenditure method is based upon figures collected from a variety of sources, such as H.M. Customs and Excise, Department of Trade and Industry enquiries and the Family Expenditure Survey.

National income accounts are published on an annual basis for the UK in the HMSO publication *United Kingdom National Accounts* (commonly referred to as the Blue Book). Apart from information at the broad aggregate level for each sector of the economy, the publication also contains detailed analyses of the various components of national income, as well as showing changes over the previous ten years. The data in this publication are of immense value to many categories of user – economists, business managers, government, international agencies and so forth (the appendix to this book lists the main sources of government statistics for the UK economy as well as the main international data sources). Some of the principle uses of national incomes statistics are:

1. To identify trends in consumer spending and industrial production.
2. To measure changes in the standard of living over time or to make comparisons between countries (commonly estimated in terms of national income per head).
3. To assist governments in formulating economic policies and plans.
4. To highlight changes in the distribution of national income between the factors of production (wages to labour, rent to property owners, and interest, profits, and dividends to the providers of capital).

It should be recognized that national income statistics are not perfect, especially as the sole basis for standard of living comparisons. As noted earlier, caution should always be exercised in using these statistics because of inevitable errors and omissions. Moreover, international comparisons are fraught with difficulties because of differences in conventions in the measurement and conversion of monetary values into a common unit of measurement. At the same time, the purchasing power of a common unit of currency may vary between countries. Also, the distribution of income, provision of state welfare services, 'quality of life' and so on must be taken into consideration when comparing average incomes per head. Ultimately, the information in national income accounts should be used alongside other indicators of economic performance and standards of living.

A model of national income determination

Equilibrium level of national income

Figure 3.1 presented diagrammatically the interrelationships between the five main sectors of the economy. This is essentially a model showing how national income in the economy is determined in terms of a circular flow of income. We now introduce the meaning of an *equilibrium* in the national economy, based on the concepts and principles already discussed. We also consider what gives rise to *disequilibrium* in the national economy.

To illustrate the main principles consider a simple model of the circular flow of income in which there is no foreign sector (what is termed a *closed economy*) and no government intervention in the economy (see Figure 3.2). It is assumed in this figure that households either save (S) or spend on consumer goods and services (C). Firms are assumed to produce goods and services for consumption (C) and investment (I). Savings in this simplified case represent a leakage from the national income flow which can be counterbalanced by firms' investment expenditure, representing an injection into the circular flow. Therefore, national income will be in equilibrium when the value of any leakages is matched by an equal value of injections. In this simple model:

$$S = I$$

i.e. Leakages = Injections

This relationship, it should be stressed, applies only in this simple model of the economy. It can, however, be extended into a more general form by including the government and foreign sectors (with the financial services sector included as an intermediary). Figure 3.3, therefore, adds the government sector, while Figure 3.4 includes the foreign sector and is the same as Figure 3.1 introduced earlier.

The effect of introducing the government sector into the circular flow is that we have another leakage from the income in the form of taxation (T). At the same time, another injection of income arises in the form of government spending (G), as shown in Figure 3.3. Now the equilibrium condition has changed so that the economy will only be in equilibrium

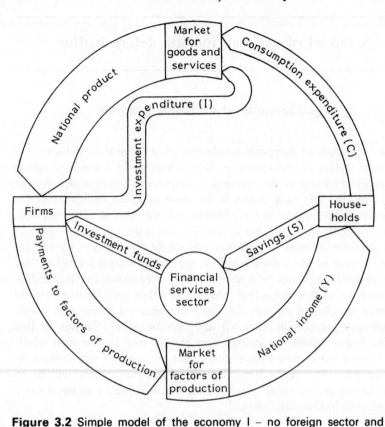

Figure 3.2 Simple model of the economy I – no foreign sector and no government sector.

when:

$$S + T = I + G$$

i.e. Leakages = Injections

Lastly, when the model is extended to an *open economy*, that is to say one with foreign trade and international capital flows, a third injection into and a third leakage from the national income emerge. When the UK buys imports or invests overseas, the expenditure represents a leakage from the domestic economy. When foreigners buy UK exports or invest in the UK these flows represent injections of income into our economy. If we denote the money value of imports and capital outflows by M and the value of exports including capital inflows by X, the general equilibrium condition

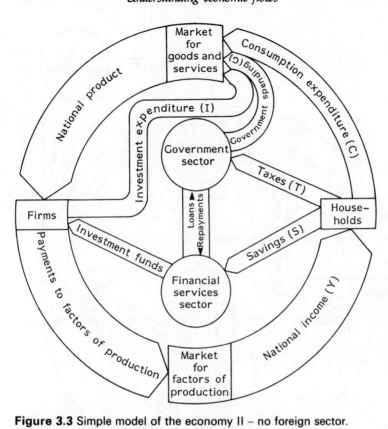

Figure 3.3 Simple model of the economy II – no foreign sector.

for national income is now written as:

$$S + T + M = I + G + X$$

i.e. Total leakages = Total injections

On the basis of this identity, we can further develop our understanding of the macroeconomy. In crude terms, equilibrium in the national income may be thought of in terms of the volume of water in a barrel. Imagine the barrel has three holes (S, T and M) and three water pipes leading into it (I, G and X) – see Figure 3.5. The level of water in the barrel will remain unchanged provided that the *total* volume of water leaking from the barrel is matched by the *total* amount flowing into it. When the total outflow equals the total inflow, the water level remains in equilibrium or balance.

An equivalent way of expressing equilibrium, but this time for an economy's national income rather than the water level in a barrel, is in

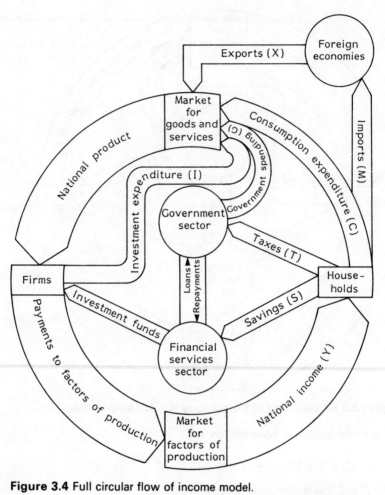

Figure 3.4 Full circular flow of income model.

terms of aggregate demand for and aggregate supply of goods and services. The equilibrium level of national income exists in an economy when:

Aggregate supply (AS) = Aggregate demand (AD)

Only when this condition is met can we state that the total value of domestic goods and services that households, government, firms and foreigners want to buy is matched by the total value of goods and services firms want to supply. Note that this refers to the demand for and supply of *domestic* goods and services (that is, including the value of exports and after deduction of expenditure on imports).

Injections

Disequilibrium:
when $(I + G + X)$ exceeds $(S+T+M)$

Equilibrium:
when $(I + G + X)$ equals $(S+T+M)$

Disequilibrium:
when $(S + T + M)$ exceeds $(I+G+X)$

Leakages

Figure 3.5 National income equilibrium – leakages and injections.

It should be appreciated that aggregate supply represents the amount of goods and services that firms are willing to produce, given the general level of wages and prices. Hence, an equilibrium national income relates to the situation where the production *plans* of firms match the *actual* supply of goods and services needed to satisfy aggregate demand in a particular time period. When this condition is satisfied there is no tendency for the economy to move away from equilibrium.

From this discussion of equilibrium it is easy to understand the meaning of a disequilibrium level of national income.

Disequilibrium level of national income

Refer back to Figure 3.5. Obviously, if the total leakage $(S + T + M)$ exceeds the total injection $(I + G + X)$, the water level will be falling. Conversely, if the total injection exceeds the total leakage then the water level must be rising. Both situations represent diequilibria since the level of water in the barrel is not constant. The same principle applies to an economy's national income. In summary, therefore, a disequilibrium level of national income occurs when the total value of leakages is greater than or less than the total value injections, i.e.:

$(S + T + M)$ is greater than $(I + G + X)$

or

$(S + T + M)$ is less than $(I + G + X)$

or, equivalently, in terms of AD and AS:

AD is greater than or less than AS

When national income is at equilibrium, there will be no tendency for prices in general to rise due to excess demand since total demand is matched by the total supply of goods and services. In addition, there will be no tendency for unemployment to rise owing to inadequate demand for the available supply of goods and services. However, in reality, economies are rarely if ever in situations of stable prices and employment levels because savings (and therefore consumer spending), taxes, investment expenditure, government expenditure, exports and imports, are all changing continuously. The real world is dominated by disequilibrium situations with rising and falling prices (inflation and deflation) and changes in the level of employment and hence unemployment.

Many economists would argue that the role of government should be to manage the macroeconomy by influencing the levels of injections and leakages and hence the degree and direction of economic activity. This may be carried out using a range of policy measures focusing upon either the demand side of the economy (adjusting the level of aggregate demand) or the supply side of the economy (affecting the total output of the economy). This gives rise to *demand management* policies and *supply-side* policies detailed in later chapters. A controversial issue in policy making today is the extent to which governments should emphasize either demand-side or supply-side measures in influencing the level of national income.

Concluding remarks

In this chapter we have discussed how national income – economic activity – is measured by the output, income and expenditure methods. We have seen that whichever method is used, the resulting totals should be identical because each method measures the same economic activity, albeit at different points in the circular flow around the economy. By focusing upon the circular flow of national income we were then able to identify certain injections into the economy and certain leakages out of it – the injections being investment, government expenditure and export revenues, and the leakages savings, taxation and import expenditure. When injections exceed leakages, like the rising water level in a barrel when more water flows in than out, the total income flowing around the economy increases. In other words, the level of economic activity rises. Conversely, when the leakages from the income flow exceed the injections into it, the level of income, and therefore the level of economic activity, falls.

Just as imbalances between the injections into and the leakages from the circular flow of income lead to changes in the level of economic activity, so it follows that an equilibrium in the level of national income will occur when the total value of injections *equals* the total value of leakages. An alternative way of looking at this is to say that an equilibrium national income level occurs when aggregate demand equals aggregate supply.

In the next chapter we develop this analysis further, initially by looking in more detail at the different components of aggregate demand and then by discussing the impact of changes in aggregate demand upon the equilibrium level of national income.

4

National income determination

The essence of national income determination

In Chapter 3 we illustrated the flows of outputs, incomes and expenditures around an economy in the form of the circular flow of income model, which is a useful diagrammatic summary of economic activity. We now turn to discuss the determination of these flows, i.e. the underlying dynamics of the macroeconomy. We are essentially interested in understanding what *causes* the level of national income to rise or fall in the short term around an economy's long-term growth path. Such fluctuations in national income give rise to what are known as business cycles in which the rate of growth in production periodically rises and falls.

This chapter considers the causes of fluctuations in national income and therefore employment and prices employing a framework developed by Keynesian economists. This forms a basis for the study of fiscal and monetary policies in the following chapters.

Keynesians versus monetarists: an overview

Economists' views on what determines national income may be broadly divided into two schools of thought: the Keynesian and the monetarist.

56

The Keynesian view

This view has evolved from the work of the Cambridge economist John Maynard Keynes, as set out in his book *The General Theory of Employment, Interest and Money* (1936). His ideas had a profound impact upon economists and governments in the post-war period and led to the concept of *Keynesian demand management*. Keynes and his followers argued that the levels of total output (aggregate supply) and employment in an economy are determined by the level of aggregate demand for goods and services. Their views were concerned largely with short-run measures to affect the level of economic activity focusing on changes in demand. Today, Keynesian economists still believe that when an economy has spare productive capacity and unemployment, investment and output can be stimulated so as to increase employment without creating inflationary pressure. They argue that this can be achieved primarily through changing government expenditure and/or taxes – that is, by what are known as *fiscal policy* measures (fiscal policy is discussed in detail in the next chapter).

The monetarist view

This view came to prominence during the early 1970s following the apparent failure of Keynesian demand management policies to bring down inflation and reduce unemployment. The monetarist approach stems largely from the work of the American economist Milton Friedman. Based partly on empirical research, initially into the historical relationship between the growth in the money supply and inflation in the USA, and partly on a theoretical study of the relationship between money supply and money GDP (the value of domestic output), Friedman argued that controlling the growth of the money supply is necessary to bring down inflation. Monetarist economists also argue that controlling inflation is a prerequisite to reducing unemployment since inflation in market economies, they believe, is harmful to private business and therefore economic growth.

Monetarist policy prescriptions, like Keynesian policy prescriptions, are directed at aggregate demand in the economy (for an alternative approach which focuses upon increasing the capacity of the economy to supply goods and services competitively – i.e. supply-side economics – see Chapter 7). However, unlike Keynesians, monetarists tend to eschew positive state action to reduce inflation and increase employment, especially through the use of fiscal measures. Instead, they prefer to rely upon private investment and free markets. In so far as government has a role to play in the economy, monetarists argue that it is to provide an environment conducive to private enterprise, including the maintenance of private property rights, establishing a framework of law which maximizes individual freedom, and controlling the growth in the money supply to prevent inflation and unexpected fluctuations in aggregate demand. Monetary policy measures are discussed in detail in Chapter 6.

The components of aggregate demand

The starting point for an analysis of fluctuations in national income is the concept of an equilibrium national income as introduced in the previous chapter. By the term equilibrium, economists mean a state of affairs in which the forces that are influencing change in opposite directions are perfectly balanced so that there is no tendency to change. Therefore, a national income equilibrium occurs when the demand for goods and services in the economy is just equal to the supply of goods and services available for purchase. There is then no tendency for the national income to rise or fall. If demand exceeds the output of goods and services, however, either output or prices, or both, will tend to rise, leading to a higher nominal value of national income. A rise in the *nominal* value of national income does not necessarily mean that the *real* value will rise: this will depend upon the economy's ability to increase output at a faster rate than any rise in prices. Similarly, if output exceeds demand either prices or output, or both, will tend to fall, leading to a decline in the nominal value of national income. Again, the real value of national income will depend upon the relative changes in output and prices. In other words, a national income equilibrium occurs when:

Aggregate supply = Aggregate demand

Aggregate supply is the total output of the economy (i.e. national income) and is commonly denoted by the letter Y. Aggregate demand is made up of a number of components as we saw in the circular flow diagrams in Chapter 3. These are consumer spending (C), investment expenditure (I), government spending (G) and exports (X). Of course, in order to calculate the demand for domestically produced goods and services, we must subtract expenditure on imports (M) since the goods bought by domestic house-holds, firms and government are likely to include a foreign component (e.g. imported raw materials). Therefore, the equilibrium condition can be expressed as:

$$Y = C + I + G + (X - M)$$

In order to understand how changes in national income (Y) may be determined by changes in aggregate demand, we must examine each of the components of aggregate demand in turn.

Consumer spending and savings

Domestic consumer spending is the dominant component of aggregate demand in all economies, dwarfing the other expenditures. For example, in 1988 in the UK, about 61 per cent of the gross domestic product was accounted for by consumption. Therefore, any changes in consumption are likely to have a significant impact upon the level of economic activity in an economy. More spending in the high street raises aggregate demand, while a fall in consumer confidence will deflate domestic spending with obvious implications for firms' sales and production. Since consumers can spend or save their income, it follows that for any given income level, when the percentage of income spent on consumer goods and services rises the level of savings falls. In contrast, a decline in the share of income spent on consumption raises the percentage of income saved.

In addition to income, a number of other factors may affect consumption, such as consumer confidence, the wealth of consumers (as reflected in savings, etc.), the availability of credit, government taxation and subsidies, advertising of goods and services and so on. Nevertheless, economists tend to single out *disposable income* as the most important influence. Disposable income (Y_d) is the amount of income that consumers have left over after paying direct taxes to the government and receiving direct state subsidies, e.g. child benefit. One way of expressing the relationship between consumer spending and disposable income is to say that an individual's total consumption (C) is dependent upon (or, to use the mathematical term, a function of – denoted by the letter f) disposable income. This is written as:

$$C = f(Y_d)$$

Also, it follows that as disposable income can be spent or saved, savings (S) are also a function of disposable income, i.e.:

$$S = f(Y_d)$$

The proportion of disposable income that goes towards consumer spending is referred to as the *average propensity to consume* (apc). In notation form:

$$apc = \frac{\text{Total consumption expenditure}}{\text{Total disposable income}} = C/Y_d$$

Similarly, the proportion of disposable income saved is known as the *average propensity to save* (aps). In notation form:

$$aps = \frac{\text{Total savings}}{\text{Total disposable income}} = S/Y_d$$

By definition, the numerical values of the average propensities to consume and save must sum to 1 since household income is either spent (consumed) or saved, i.e.:

$$apc + aps = 1$$

When total disposable income rises in an economy, and since consumption and savings are related to income, total consumer spending and savings will also increase. Similarly, when total disposable income falls, spending and savings will decline. The proportion of any increase in disposable income which is spent on consumer goods and services is known as the *marginal propensity to consume* (mpc), while that part of any increase which is absorbed by extra savings is referred to as the *marginal propensity to save* (mps). More formally:

$$mpc = \frac{\text{Change in consumption expenditure}}{\text{Change in disposable income}} = \Delta C/\Delta Y_d$$

$$mps = \frac{\text{Change in savings}}{\text{Change in disposable income}} = \Delta S/\Delta Y_d$$

where Δ is a shorthand notation for 'a small change in'.

Once again, since household income can only be used for consumption or savings, it follows that the numerical values of the marginal propensities to consume and save must sum to 1, i.e.:

$$mpc + mps = 1$$

An example might help to clarify the meaning of the terms apc, aps, mpc and mps. Suppose, for instance, that an individual household spends

72 per cent of its total disposable income of £500 on consumer goods (i.e. C = £360) and saves the rest (S = £140). If the household's disposable income now rises to £600, it might decide to spend £60 of the extra £100, saving the remainder. Initially, the apc was 0.72 (i.e. £360/£500) and the aps 0.28 (i.e. £140/£500) but now the apc is 0.7 (i.e. £420/£600) and the aps is 0.3 (i.e. £180/£600). The mpc and mps can also be calculated. The mpc is 0.6 (= £60/£100) and the mps 0.4 (= £40/£100).

This example illustrates a tendency that Keynes believed affected all economies: over the long-term, as disposable incomes rise, people tend to save a larger proportion of any increase in income (note that although this may not be true for all individuals, all that is being argued is that it will tend to be true for the economy as a whole). In other words, the mpc, and therefore the apc, tend to fall. By similar logic we can deduce that different income groups in society at any given time can be expected to have different propensities to consume and save. In general, we would expect richer social groups to save a larger percentage of any increase in disposable income than poorer groups.

At present, for the UK as a whole, the mpc is estimated to be around 0.9 and the mps 0.1. This figure will, of course, be influenced over time by a number of factors such as changes in the distribution of income (the impact of taxes and state welfare payments), the availability of credit, interest paid on savings, and the age distribution of the population (the young and the retired tend to spend a large proportion of their incomes on consumption, whereas middle-aged people usually have a higher propensity to save).

Also, many economists question whether consumption and savings are directly linked to current disposable incomes. Consumption and savings may not react immediately to changes in income. For instance, people may draw on past savings to maintain consumption when current disposable incomes fall, say in the early stages of an economic recession, particularly if they believe that their incomes will subsequently recover. This leads to the idea that consumption is dependent upon people's perceptions of their lifetime (or permanent) incomes rather than their current disposable incomes. In which case, consumption may not react immediately to changes in income during cyclical fluctuations in economy activity. In economic upturns consumption will tend to lag behind the rise in income, while in economic downturns the rate of consumption will not fall as quickly as the fall in the growth rate of incomes. The exact nature of the relationship between consumption and current income continues to be researched and the Keynesian view about the mpc, in particular, is challenged. Nevertheless, to assume that consumption is dependent simply upon current disposable income and that the mpc falls or stays constant as incomes rise

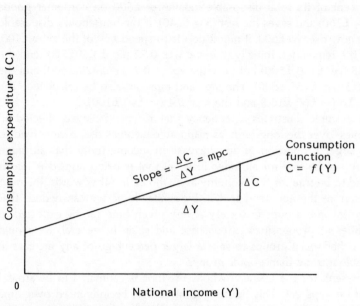

Figure 4.1 The consumption function.

is satisfactory for the overview of national income determination that we are developing in this chapter.

The relationship between total consumer expenditure and national income can be shown diagrammatically – see Figure 4.1. This relationship is known as the *consumption function* and plays an important role in Keynesian economics. It will be noted that, for simplicity, we have assumed that consumption (and hence savings) has a constant relationship with national income and is thus shown as a straight line (the mpc is therefore assumed to be constant given by the slope of the consumption function). We have also assumed that there is no direct taxation, i.e. that C is related to total income instead of disposable income. This is a common assumption used merely to simplify the analysis.

Investment expenditure

Private investment is another major component of aggregate demand, accounting for 22 per cent of UK gross domestic product in 1988. The

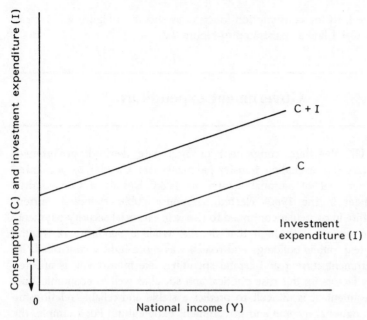

Figure 4.2 Consumption and investment.

relationship between investment expenditure and national income, how-ever, is far more complex than the relationship between consumption expenditure and national income. In practice, investment expenditure decisions by firms in the private sector are likely to be dependent upon a host of factors such as: interest rates, return on capital, technology, the growth in consumer demand, taxation and investment incentives, business confidence and expectations, as well as the level of and changes in national income itself. Given this complexity, it does not seem unreasonable to argue, as many economists have done as a simplifying assumption, that investment (I) is largely *independent* of the level of national income. In Keynesian analysis of economic fluctuations, in particular, the emphasis tends to be more upon the effects on investment of changes in business confidence than changes in national income as such.

If investment is treated as being independent of national income levels then we can illustrate this by graphing the level of investment as a straight line parallel to the national income axis as in Figure 4.2. The amount of investment, I, is determined by the other possible factors affecting investment already referred to, such that when any of these change, investment rises or falls as appropriate: i.e. the investment line shifts up or down. Moreover, if we add the actual amount of investment in the economy, I, to the consumption function as shown in Figure 4.1, we can derive a C + I line as illustrated in Figure 4.2.

Government expenditure

In the UK the third component of aggregate demand, government expenditure (G), excluding transfer payments (see Chapter 3), accounted for 22 per cent of national income in 1988. Despite a Conservative government in the 1980s elected to reduce public spending, current expenditure in particular continued to rise (e.g. on social security payments including pensions) through that decade, while expenditure on capital account (e.g. public buildings and roads) was more tightly controlled.

Government current and capital spending, like investment, is affected by many factors (in this case political and social as well as economic) and, like investment, it is difficult to predict a stable and reliable relationship between national income and government expenditure. For example, the introduction of a new road-building or school-building programme is much

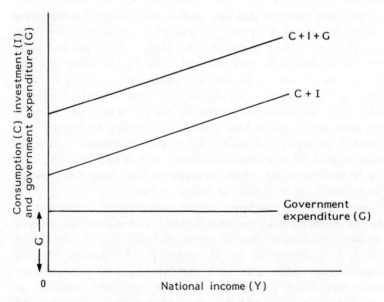

Figure 4.3 Consumption, investment and government expenditure.

more likely to be influenced by traffic density and the numbers of schoolchildren than national income. Also, it is not clear what will happen to government spending when national income fluctuates. For instance, when the growth in national income falls, governments might attempt to reign back their spending so as to avoid a rise in the tax burden. On the other hand, economic recessions lead to higher unemployment and more social deprivation, which tend to increase public spending.

Given the uncertainty about how government spending will change as national income changes, we shall assume that G, like investment, is independent of national income, at least for the sake of illustration. It is therefore shown as a horizontal line in Figure 4.3, with G representing the total value of government spending. Should government expenditure rise or fall for whatever reason, unrelated to a change in national income, this will be reflected in the diagram by a parallel shift upwards or downwards in the line. Moreover, adding G to C and I gives the line C + I + G as shown in Figure 4.3.

Export and import expenditure

We can now complete our analysis of aggregate demand by adding the difference between expenditure on exports (X) and imports (M) to C + I + G. When foreigners buy British exports, take holidays in Britain or travel with British Airways for example, the amount remitted to the UK becomes part of the total demand for UK goods and services. Similarly, when people in Britain buy foreign goods, holidays abroad and use foreign airlines for example, income leaks out of the UK circular flow of income (in the way explained in Chapter 3) and is lost to the UK economy (except that these funds in turn permit people in other countries to buy our exports, see Chapter 8). In the same way, any flows of funds into the country for investment purposes, including investments in stocks and shares, bank accounts and more tangible investments such as the building of new offices and factories, add to demand here. In contrast, when UK residents invest overseas this takes funds out of the UK, thereby adding to demand abroad but reducing it in the UK. Therefore, here we define the terms exports and imports widely to include not just the flows of goods and services but also capital flows into and out of the economy.

We shall assume for convenience that X and M, like I and G, are independent of national income, although this is a gross simplification.

Export levels for goods and services are usually more related to the level of incomes in export markets than domestic national income, but booming demand at home may lead to potential exports being diverted to the home market producing an inverse relationship between domestic national income and exports. At the same time, capital inflows may rise as an economy expands, implying that this component of exports is directly related to national income. Turning to imports, we tend to buy more imported goods and services as our incomes rise; while the effect of rising domestic incomes on capital outflows is difficult to predict. In general, although exports and imports may be affected by changes in national income, the precise relationship is quite complex. Hence, rather than pursue this further we shall assume that X and M are independent of national income. Once again, such a simplifying assumption allows us to make progress without detracting from the significance of the discussion.

The difference between X and M can be positive or negative depending upon whether the value of exports is greater or less than the value of imports. Assuming that it is positive, adding X − M to C, I and G gives the aggregate demand schedule as shown in Figure 4.4, illustrating the

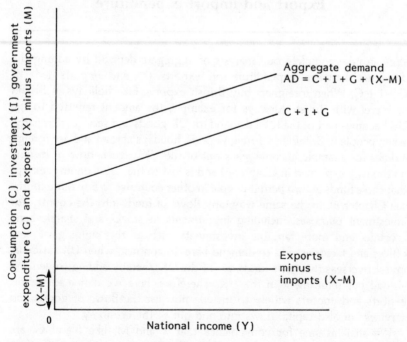

Figure 4.4 Aggregate demand schedule.

relationship between total expenditure in the economy and national income. In this figure the vertical distance between the lines C + I + G (as derived above) and C + I + G + (X − M) represents the net value of UK exports and imports. Therefore, if imports were greater than exports, the C + I + G + (X − M) line would lie below the C + I + G line.

Deflationary and inflationary gaps

Having considered each category of aggregate demand and its relationship to national income, we can now develop Keynesian analysis further and, in particular, look at the circumstances in which an equilibrium national income equates with unemployment or inflation. It will be recalled from the above discussion and Chapter 3 that equilibrium in an economy exists when aggregate demand equals aggregate supply so that there are no forces making for a change in national income. We have shown that aggregate demand (AD) is given by C + I + G + (X − M) and that aggregate supply represents the total output of the economy and is therefore the same as the national income (Y). Therefore, as a condition of equilibrium we can write:

$$Y = AD = C + I + G + (X − M)$$

If values of Y and AD are graphed together, then equilibrium positions of the economy will be shown along a 45° line (assuming the same scales are used on both axes) (see Figure 4.5). In other words, any point along this 45° line represents an equality between the level of national income (i.e. output or aggregate supply) and the level of aggregate demand.

Superimposing the aggregate demand schedule in Figure 4.4 onto this diagram allows us to identify what level of equilibrium activity in the economy exists at any particular point in time. This is shown in Figure 4.6, where the equilibrium national income is at Y_e. This is the only level of aggregate demand where the economy is in equilibrium. Movement towards other levels of aggregate demand would lead to a rise or fall in national income. For example, point A on the aggregate demand line indicates an aggregate demand greater than aggregate supply and is therefore not an equilibrium point. Similarly, point B indicates an aggregate demand which is less than the aggregate supply. Again, this cannot represent an equilibrium level of national income. Remember that while the line AD shows all the levels of aggregate demand in relation to different

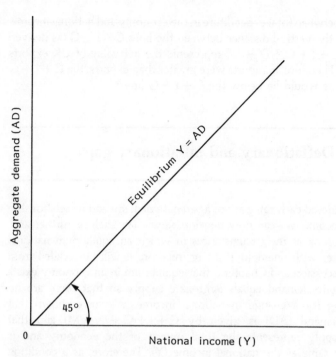

Figure 4.5 Equilibrium level of national income.

national income levels, only where AD = AS can there be an equilibrium level of national income and this must be where the AD line crosses the 45° line – the 45° line having been drawn to show all equilibrium points where AD = AS.

Using this type of analysis it is easy to show how the economy could be stable or in equilibrium either at low or high levels of economic activity. Low economic activity implies unemployment of the nation's resources, while high economic activity implies that the economy is operating near to or at full employment. This gives rise to the notion of *deflationary* and *inflationary gaps* respectively.

Deflationary and inflationary gaps

A deflationary gap is the amount by which aggregate demand must be increased to raise the equilibrium level of national income (Y_e) to its full employment level (Y_f). Conversely, an inflationary gap shows the amount by which AD must be decreased in order to bring the equilibrium income down from Y_e to Y_f with stable prices. Both of these possibilities are shown in Figure 4.7. In the case of Figure 4.7(a), the equilibrium level of national income is to the left of that level which would ensure full

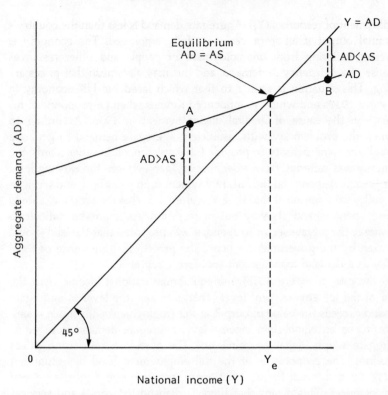

Figure 4.6 Aggregate demand and equilibrium level of national income.

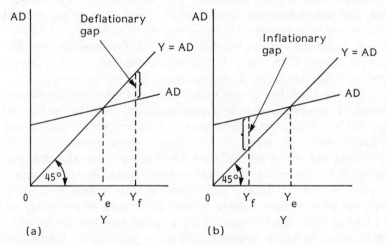

Figure 4.7 (a) Deflationary and (b) inflationary gaps.

employment of resources (Y_f). Aggregate demand is less than the country's potential output if all resources were fully employed. The economy is therefore suffering from unemployment of people and other resources because of a deficiency in demand, and this may also mean that prices are falling. This situation is similar to that which faced the UK economy in the early 1930s and which so influenced Keynes when he propounded his theory on the cause of general unemployment in 1936. According to Keynes, the problem lay with insufficient aggregate demand to generate enough economic activity to provide full employment. In other words, the economy was suffering from a deflationary gap between the existing level of aggregate demand and the full employment supply of goods and services. His policy prescription at that time, therefore, was that the economy should 'spend, spend, spend' its way out of recession. As it proved difficult to encourage the private sector to spend, it was proposed that the lead should be taken by the government – hence the growth in significance of fiscal policy as a demand management tool (see Chapter 5).

In the case of Figure 4.7(b), the equilibrium national income is to the right of the full employment level. That is to say, the level of aggregate demand exceeds the value of output at full employment with stable prices. Since, to be an equilibrium income level aggregate demand must equal aggregate supply, what is going on? The answer lies in rising prices (inflation). The economy is at the full employment level of output but excess demand, equal to the inflationary gap, is pushing up the general level of prices. This means that there is demand for goods and services that has been satisfied only by raising prices.

Neither deflationary nor inflationary gaps are desirable, so an obvious further question is how can these gaps be closed so as to achieve full employment with stable prices? In answering this question there is a division between economists and policy-makers. Indeed, this question arguably raises the biggest controversy in macroeconomics today: the necessary degree of state intervention in the management of the economy.

On the one hand, free market economists (who are often monetarists, although by no means all monetarists are passionate about the free market) argue that private enterprise in conjunction with competitive markets will eventually restore an equilibrium level of national income with full employment and low or zero inflation. The free market is self-regulating, therefore state intervention is at best unnecessary and at worst hampers the operation of market forces. On the other hand, Keynesians (incidentally along with other groups, notably Marxist economists, whose views are not explored in this book) dispute that the market economy can be relied upon to adjust to full employment with stable prices. Either the process will not occur at all or, if it does, it will take too long and have unacceptable social and political consequences. Writing at a time of protracted unemployment, Keynes dismissed waiting for market adjustments, observing succinctly: 'in the long-run we are all dead'.

Adopting a Keynesian stance (we consider monetarist and free market views in more detail in Chapters 6 and 7), if free market forces are not capable of regulating the level of economic activity, then there is a clear case for state intervention. This leads to a subsidiary question concerning how governments might attempt to influence economic activity in order to close deflationary and inflationary gaps in aggregate demand. In other words, how can aggregate demand be raised in an economy to reverse deflationary pressures or to squeeze out inflationary pressures?

Keynesian economists assign the responsibility for managing aggregate demand to government, using *fiscal policy* measures especially, which may involve either or both of the following:

1. Changes in personal taxation to influence consumer spending directly and therefore aggregate demand.
2. Changes in government spending, again to influence aggregate demand directly.

In addition to using fiscal policy to influence consumption and change government spending, other possibilities recognized by Keynesians involve affecting the level of private investment and the flow of exports and imports. For example, since 1945 various UK governments under the influence of Keynesian precepts have introduced investment incentives, changed interest rates in a countercyclical fashion, offered export inducements from time to time, and have resorted to tariffs and quotas to limit spending on imports (such attempts by governments to moderate economic activity in the post-war period in a Keynesian fashion were known as 'stop–go' or fine-tuning policies).

Keynesian economists stress that initial changes in investment, government spending and export and import revenues have a multiple impact upon changes in national income and that this effect can be broadly estimated. This gives rise to one of the most important concepts in Keynesian macroeconomic analysis with regard to the measurement of the impact of changes in aggregate demand, namely the *multiplier*.

Measuring the impact of changes in aggregate demand: the multiplier

Changes in any of the components of aggregate demand will have an effect on the equilibrium level of national income (Y_e). For example, a change in any of the injections into or leakages from the circular flow of income will bring about a change in the level of Y. As we have already discussed, injections refer to either government spending (G), investment spending (I) or export revenues (X), which add to the circular flow; while leakages refer to taxation (T), savings (S) or import revenues (M), which reduce the amount of income circulating around the economy.

Let us consider a change in one of the injections. For example, if the government decides to raise its level of expenditure then, by definition, aggregate demand in the economy will increase, as shown in Figure 4.8. The increase in G is depicted as a vertical movement in aggregate demand from AD_1 to AD_2. Therefore, an initial increase in government expenditure has given rise to a new equilibrium level of national income Y_e^*. It is important to notice, however, that the initial increase in government expenditure is less than the consequent increase in national income. This is a fundamental point of Keynesian analysis. In general, a small initial increase in aggregate demand leads to a larger total increase in national income. The extent to which Y changes as a result of a change in an injection or leakage is measured by the *national income multiplier*.

The multiplier effect is defined as *the ratio of the resultant change in national income to the initial change in injections or leakages*. This gives rise to measures such as the government expenditure multiplier ($\Delta Y/\Delta G$), investment multiplier ($\Delta Y/\Delta I$) and the export multiplier ($\Delta Y/\Delta X$), where, as before, Δ means 'change in'. Similarly, we can measure the multiplier effects of changes in any of the leakages, i.e. $\Delta Y/\Delta T$, $\Delta Y/\Delta S$ and $\Delta Y/\Delta M$. In more general terms:

$$\text{Size of the multiplier} = \frac{\text{Change in national income}}{\text{Initial change in aggregate demand}}$$

From Figure 4.8 it should be clear that the value of the multiplier is dependent upon the slope of the aggregate demand line. In our simplified example, this slope is equal to the marginal propensity to consume (mpc) since the other components of aggregate demand (G, I and X − M) have

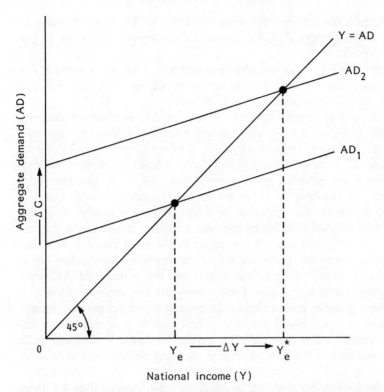

Figure 4.8 The impact of increasing government expenditure upon aggregate demand.

been assumed to be unrelated to national income. In this simple case, therefore, the impact of any change in aggregate demand will depend upon the size of the leakage from the circular flow of income in the form of savings. That is, the multiplier will depend upon the mps and may be measured as:

Multiplier $= 1/\text{mps}$

This is equivalent to $1/(1 - \text{mpc})$ since the mpc + mps = 1 (as noted on page 60). However, in addition to savings the other two leakages from the circular flow (taxation and expenditure on imports) generally affect the size of the multiplier. In this case the formula for the multiplier is a little more complicated, being defined as:

Multiplier $= 1/(\text{mps} + \text{mpm} + \text{mpt})$

where mps is the marginal propensity to save, $\Delta S/\Delta Y$; mpm the marginal propensity to import, $\Delta M/\Delta Y$; and mpt the marginal propensity to pay taxes, $\Delta T/\Delta Y$.

A 'demultiplier' effect will also arise when we have a reduction in any of the injections I, G and X. A reduction in aggregate demand will lead to a multiplied reduction in national income.

Recalling the circular flow of income model, summarized diagrammatically in Figure 3.1, we can visualize an initial addition to aggregate demand going around the economy, but as it does so some of the additional spending is lost to the circular flow because it leaks out through savings, expenditure on imported goods and services, and to the government in the form of taxation. In other words, the amount of extra spending circulating around the economy for a second time is smaller (than that which was injected initially) by the amount which leaked out in the first round. Similarly, the amount circulating in the third round is less than that which circulated in the second by the amount which leaked out in the second round, and so on. Therefore, the amount of additional expenditure circulating around the economy declines continuously until it becomes negligible. If we added up the amount of extra demand or income generated in each round we should find that it is a multiple of the initial injection – this multiple being smaller the larger the leakages from the circular flow in the form of savings, spending on imports and taxation. The total increase in income in relation to the initial increase in expenditure is the multiplier. So that, for instance, if total income rises by twice the initial expenditure then the multiplier has a value of two.

The multiplier effect is often likened to throwing a stone into the centre of a lake, causing ripples which spread throughout the water. The ripples are greatest at the centre but diminish nearer the banks. This gives rise to the notion of 'regional' as well as national multiplier effects with the leakage of income into imports now defined as spending outside of the region in question. For example, a new government shipbuilding order for Barrow-in-Furness would probably have its greatest impact upon national income in the surrounding area, especially in terms of increased employment and therefore expenditure in local shops and clubs. However, other areas further afield would also benefit from new shipyard orders and the increased spending power of the shipyard workers. The larger the spending on goods and services outside the Barrow-in-Furness area the smaller the regional multiplier effect of the new shipbuilding order. Since 'imports' include all spending outside of the region, the smaller the region, the smaller the multiplier. For this reason, national income multipliers can be expected to be larger than regional income multipliers.

The importance of the national income multiplier

The analysis so far may seem somewhat remote from the real world of business managers. Diagrams with 45° lines, consumption functions, equilibrium national incomes and national income multipliers are not part of the normal vocabulary of business; nor do they appear often in press reporting of economic events. However, they are important concepts if we are really to understand how an economy functions. It is one thing, for example, to read in the financial columns that the rate of growth of the economy is falling, it is quite another to appreciate the full significance of this – both in terms of why it is declining and the implications for business. In particular, changes in aggregate demand have direct and powerful effects on the business sector in terms of output and profits, aggravated by the multiplier effect. A sound understanding and awareness of likely changes in economic activity is essential if firms are to plan their production levels and their marketing strategies successfully.

In addition, many industries are affected directly by private and public sector investment programmes, both local and national. In this context, an appreciation of multiplier effects is of immense value in helping to plan ahead. For example, decisions by the government to build new roads have a significant impact upon directly related industrial sectors such as the various construction industries. But there are also likely to be important knock-on effects from large investment programmes for the rest of the economy. A current example is the building of the Channel Tunnel which is expected to have far-reaching effects on employment levels and output throughout the whole of the UK, and especially with regard to the local economy in the south-east.

Not only can businesses gain from an understanding of the multiplier process, it also provides a simple but useful quantitative guide for the government in assessing the impact of policy measures upon the economy. Government economic policies may even be directed at influencing the size of the multiplier itself, and hence aggregate demand, through effecting changes in the rate of taxation, the level of savings and the flow of imports.

Governments usually resort to demand management when the economy is in danger of 'overheating', that is when domestic demand exceeds the ability of the economy to supply goods and services, thereby aggravating inflation and attracting imports. Similarly, in the case of downturns in economic activity, the government may decide to intervene and stimulate aggregate demand to boost output. In both cases, in deciding by how much demand should be lowered or raised in order to reduce or increase national income to the desired level, account must be taken of the multiplier effects. For example, if the government estimates that demand must decline by £4m to bring down inflation, and the multiplier effect of government spending is estimated to be two, then government spending needs only to be reduced by £2m for the target to be achieved. Indeed, if government spending was reduced by the full £4m and the multiplier remained at two, the result would be a severe and unintended collapse in aggregate demand and national income of £8m.

The use of Keynesian demand management policies is further illustrated below with respect to *business cycles*. In order to appreciate this topic more fully, however, we shall first introduce another important economic concept concerning the impact of changes in expenditure upon national income, known as the accelerator principle.

The accelerator principle

The accelerator principle relates to *changes* in the level of investment in an economy and, more specifically, to the impact of changes in consumption upon investment. A small increase in the output of consumer goods and services tends to lead to a larger increase in the production of capital equipment needed to produce those goods. This change in output in the capital goods industry then has an impact upon the economy by accelerating the pace of growth – hence the name. The accelerator can also work in reverse. A small decline in demand for consumer goods and services tends to lead to the shelving of investment plans, which in turn provokes a fall in orders for capital equipment and ultimately a downturn in the rate of economic growth.

A brief example might help to clarify the accelerator principle. Suppose that a firm manufactures goods using ten machines, each of which produces 1,000 units per annum. Also suppose that the total demand for the firm's output is currently 10,000 units per annum. To simplify the discussion we will assume no depreciation, therefore all investment expands capacity. Now, if demand remained at 10,000 units per annum, no investment would take place; but if demand rose to, say, 12,000 units then two new machines would be ordered to produce the extra output. If subsequently demand rose again, this time to 15,000 units, a further three machines would be purchased and so forth. Note that the 3,000 rise in demand represents a 25 per cent increase in the output of goods, while the three extra machines amounts to a 50 per cent rise in the production of the machine manufacturing industry. Hence the rise in consumer demand has caused an accelerated increase in the demand for new machines. Equally, of course, if at some stage demand ceased to grow then the firm would cease investing and again a small fall in consumer demand would trigger a much larger proportionate fall in the demand for machines.

This process by which investment jumps as consumer demand rises and then collapses when the growth in demand ends can be observed in all economies and makes the state of new orders for the engineering industry a good barometer of changes in the overall level of economic activity. Specifically, the accelerator principle highlights the following:

1. Net investment by a firm will be maintained only if the demand for the firm's output continues to rise at a steady rate.
2. Demand for consumer goods and services must increase *at an increasing rate* if net investment is to rise.
3. When demand ceases to grow then net investment becomes zero.

In practice, the accelerator principle does not work quite so mechanically as set out above. In particular, investment decisions are also affected by business expectations: for example, businesses may continue to invest during a downturn in consumer demand if they feel it is temporary and that investment is necessary if they are to compete successfully in the future. Similarly, if a firm is working with excess capacity, an increase in consumer demand might be met out of this excess capacity rather than through new investment. Nevertheless, the accelerator effect operates in economies, albeit in a crude way, and is important in an understanding of the causes of economic fluctuations. More particularly, the accelerator emphasizes the interrelationships between income, consumer demand, investment and the business cycle. Since a change in consumer demand is largely dependent upon a change in national income (Y) from one time period to the next, and investment (I) is affected by changes in consumer demand, the accelerator principle in its most simple form can be expressed as:

$$I = a\Delta Y$$

where I is current investment expenditure, a the accelerator effect, and ΔY the change in national income between the current and previous time period. In other words, the level of investment is related to changes in income over time by the accelerator process.

The business cycle

The business (or trade) cycle is the term used by economists to describe the continual ups and downs in the rate of growth of national income experienced since the Industrial Revolution. Economists in the nineteenth century first became aware of fairly regular cycles of economic activity in industrial economies, many lasting between seven and ten years – although the precise length of cycles has proven as controversial as the different explanations that have been put forward as to their cause. The English economist William Stanley Jevons propounded in the 1870s a theory of business cycles based upon sun spots affecting harvests – an idea of little moment except that it generated a search for a more satisfactory explanation. In subsequent decades cycles were linked with expansions and contractions in credit and later, in Keynesian analysis, with the multiplier and the accelerator processes.

Each business cycle is associated with a *boom* period in which consumer demand is rising quickly and investment and business profits are high. This is followed by a period of *recession* when the growth in consumer demand and profitability slows down and investment, production and employment are reduced. The third phase involves a period of trade *slump* in which there is heavy unemployment, unused industrial capacity, stable or falling prices and low business confidence. Eventually, however, the slump phase turns into a period of economic *recovery* as investment and employment pick up and business confidence returns. In turn, this leads to a new boom period and the cycle begins all over again. This pattern of economic activity is illustrated in Figure 4.9.

Keynes argued that the multiplier and accelerator effects combined explained the nature of business cycles. If firms face an increase in actual demand (or even expected demand) that cannot be met from existing capacity, they will invest in more capital equipment. Since additional investment expenditure (I) is an injection into the circular flow of income, the level of national income (Y) will rise and by more than the initial increase in investment because of the multiplier effect. The rise in national income itself stimulates a further rise in consumption expenditure (C), which leads to more investment through the accelerator process, and so on. The interrelationship between the accelerator and the multiplier effects in business cycles can be summarized as follows:

$$\Delta C \rightarrow a\Delta I \rightarrow k\Delta Y \rightarrow \Delta C \rightarrow a\Delta I \ldots$$

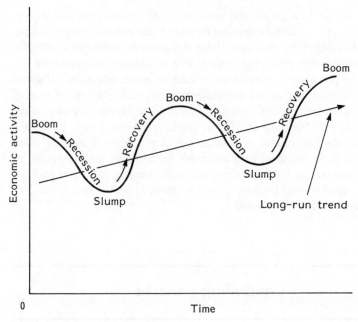

Figure 4.9 The business cycle.

where *a* denotes the accelerator effect and *k* the multiplier effect. In relation to Figure 4.9 an initial rise in investment leads to higher incomes through the multiplier effect. The rise in income in turn leads to more consumer demand and, through the accelerator effect, a further increase in the pace of investment, and so on. This process occurs in the recovery and boom phases of the business cycle. Similarly, during the recession and slump stages a reduction in investment leads to a fall in incomes, less consumer demand, more cancelled investment programmes and so forth, with the multiplier and accelerator effects working in reverse. Together the multiplier and accelerator effects exaggerate the economic consequences of any initial small changes in demand.

Less obvious, perhaps, is why a boom, once it is underway, comes to an end or why, once an economy goes into a slump, the end result is not total economic collapse. The explanation lies in *turning points* in the business cycle. In a period of economic expansion economic bottlenecks eventually emerge, notably shortages of labour, raw materials and perhaps energy. In addition, high investment may increase the cost of credit (interest rates). The overall effect is to drive up the costs of firms' inputs. The rise in costs in turn pushes up output prices leading eventually to a fall in the rate of growth of demand for goods and services. Higher prices may also lead to government action to deflate demand through fiscal and monetary measures to prevent accelerating inflation. These deflationary pressures eventually affect demand in the economy, leading to a slowdown in investment.

A turning point also occurs when economies are in recession. Although businesses will initially cancel investments when trade slackens, it is very unlikely that investment will contract to zero. Some investment must occur if production is to continue at all over the longer term, if only to replace the existing stock of capital as it wears out (depreciates). Therefore, there will be a floor to the level of investment. In addition, after a period of economic contraction cost pressures, including interest rates and perhaps wage rates, tend to ease leading to new business opportunities. Eventually the economic decline is reversed.

Concluding remarks

In this chapter we have considered both how an equilibrium level of national income is determined and the Keynesian notion of an equilibrium level of national income below or above the economy's full employment level. We looked, in particular, at the composition of aggregate demand and the effect of changes in aggregate demand on national income and therefore employment and inflation. Especially important is the process by which changes in aggregate demand affect the economy through the multiplier and accelerator effects. Together these effects provide key insights into the nature of the business cycle and fluctuations in economic activity.

In the next chapter we turn to the use of fiscal policy by governments to smooth out economic fluctuations arising from the business cycle. Can governments, by changing taxes and public spending, offset the effects on the level of economic activity of fluctuations in private sector consumption and investment expenditure so that the economy can be maintained at full employment with stable prices? In the post-war period, Keynesian economists thought they could. Today, however, many economists are sceptical on theoretical grounds and because of the experience of economic management in the post-war years. Indeed, some economists challenge the core feature of Keynesian economics – the notion of an equilibrium national income with unemployment (at least over the long term) in market economies. They prefer to emphasize that in competitive, free market economies all goods and services should be sold and all labour employed through variations in wages and prices. Therefore, there is no need for state interference in the form of aggregate demand management using fiscal policy. Indeed, some argue that state interference is a principle *cause* of inflation and unemployment because it undermines the smooth operation of the market economy. These ideas are explored in Chapters 6 and 7.

5

Management of the economy I: Fiscal policy

The essence of fiscal policy

In Chapter 4 demand management was defined as government policy measures directed at attempting to influence the level of aggregate demand (AD) in the economy and hence the level of economic activity. In this chapter, we shall examine the importance of a particular type of policy in this context, namely fiscal policy. The idea of using fiscal policy for demand management stems largely from the work of the Cambridge economist John Maynard Keynes in the 1930s and is concerned with manipulating taxation (personal and/or corporate) and government expenditure to influence the level of economic activity. Remember that an increase in government expenditure (G) is referred to as an *injection* into the circular flow of income. Hence, an increase in G will expand aggregate demand and, if the economy has sufficient spare capacity to meet this extra demand, physical production (i.e. *real* national income) and employment will also increase. In contrast, taxation is referred to as a *leakage*, such that an increase in taxes will reduce aggregate demand and the level of economic activity (similarly, a cut in government expenditure or a reduction in taxation will have opposite effects on the economy to those just outlined).

In the previous chapter we also identified how inflationary and deflationary gaps between aggregate demand and full employment output with stable prices could arise. Keynes was particularly concerned with the deflationary gap when he wrote *The General Theory of Employment, Interest*

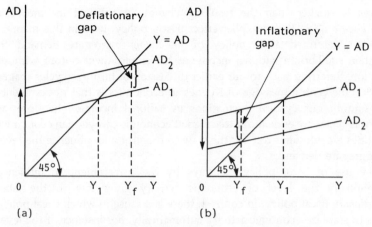

Figure 5.1 Closing (a) deflationary and (b) inflationary gaps.

and Money (1936). The 1930s were a time of high unemployment. In the post-war years, however, Keynesian economists were more concerned with keeping down inflation. Keynes had argued that government spending and taxation levels could be used to eliminate a deflationary gap in the economy. The resulting rise in public or private spending could produce a sustained rise in economic activity. Keynesians argued that an inflationary gap could be removed in a similar way by provoking a fall in public or private spending.

To close a deflationary gap (where the equilibrium level of national income is below the full employment level) and thus increase aggregate demand to the level required to raise national income, the government could either raise government expenditure or reduce taxation levels. Either of these measures would produce a multiple rise in demand through the *multiplier* effect discussed in Chapter 4. In contrast, to close an inflationary gap (where the equilibrium level of national income exceeds the full employment level), the government could either reduce government expenditure or raise taxation levels. Again these measures, Keynesians argued, would have the effect of reducing aggregate demand, this time through a negative multiplier effect. Figure 5.1 illustrates both cases.

In Figure 5.1(a) fiscal measures cause aggregate demand to rise from AD_1 to AD_2 leading to an increase in national income from Y_1 to Y_f. In Figure 5.1(b) the level of aggregate demand is reduced from AD_1 to AD_2 leading to a decrease in national income from Y_1 to Y_f. In both cases Y_f represents an equilibrium level of national income with full employment and stable prices. Also, note that the change in aggregate demand in both figures is smaller than the resulting change in national income. The difference reflects the multiplier effect. Fiscal policy, used in this manner, is often described as a policy of *fine-tuning* aggregate demand to maintain equilibrium national income at full employment output without inflation. Referring back to our earlier discussion of business cycles (pages 78–80), the central message of Keynesian economics is that governments can smooth out cyclical fluctuations in national income. Therefore, as business cycles are endemic to free market economies, Keynesian economics identifies a continuing role for the state to monitor and influence the level of aggregate demand.

The use of fiscal policy measures by the government to influence intentionally the level of economic activity gives rise to the label *discretionary* fiscal policy. In contrast, there is a sense in which fiscal policy helps to stabilize economic activity automatically. For instance, if the level of unemployment rises, tax revenue to the government will tend to decline (income tax revenues will fall as incomes contract and less spending leads to lower VAT receipts), while government expenditure on the various forms of welfare benefits will rise, unless the government takes positive steps to stop this happening. The fall in tax revenue represents a reduction in a leakage from the circular flow of income, while the increase in government spending represents a larger injection into the circular flow. Combined, these effects result in aggregate demand falling less quickly than in the absence of government involvement in the economy. Fiscal policy in this context is referred to as an *automatic stabilizer*, i.e. there has been no deliberate action on the part of the government to alleviate any fall in aggregate demand due to rising unemployment but it occurs automatically once the change in economic activity takes place.

Problems with fine-tuning aggregate demand

In the post-war period through to the mid-1970s a number of western countries, especially the UK, attempted to fine-tune aggregate demand using fiscal policy (often coupled with some monetary measures such as changes in interest rates – see the discussion of monetary policy in the next chapter). Up to the late 1960s UK unemployment remained low in most years, which seems to suggest that the policy was successful. On the other hand, the reconstruction of the continental European economies after the war, with more international economic co-operation for example with regard to exchange rates (see the discussion of exchange rates in Chapter 9), and increased free trade supervised by the General Agreement on Tariffs and Trade (GATT) signed in 1947, led to an unparalleled expansion in world trade from which the UK benefited. The extent, therefore, to which low unemployment was the product of Keynesian fine-tuning remains controversial. Certainly in the 1970s, both unemployment and inflation rose leading to *stagflation* which Keynesian economics appeared unable to tackle through fiscal measures alone. From a Keynesian viewpoint, to reverse rising unemployment requires reducing taxes and increasing government spending to boost aggregate demand. Higher inflation, in contrast, requires the opposite, that is higher taxation and reduced public spending to lower total demand in the economy. Clearly, both policies cannot be pursued at the same time.

One possible solution, much favoured by Keynesian economists in the 1960s and 1970s and pursued by governments at that time, was the introduction of a *prices and incomes policy*. The idea was that inflation could be confined by voluntary or mandatory limits on wage and price increases, while at the same time fiscal measures were used to support employment. The history of prices and incomes policies in the UK is not, however, a happy one. While they succeeded initially in restraining wage demands, they eventually broke down as workers refused to accept a reduction in real incomes. This breakdown led to a wage–price explosion, which occurred most dramatically in the coal miners' strike of 1974 and the 'winter of discontent' of 1978–9. The failure of prices and incomes policies to provide much more than a breathing space in the battle against inflation is not too surprising when we recall that they merely hold down cost increases coming from wages. They do nothing to tackle other sources of inflation, for example excess aggregate demand resulting from high public spending.

As a means of fine-tuning aggregate demand, government spending and taxation were limited in their effects for a number of reasons:

1. The full impact of government spending programmes (such as in the case of major capital projects) often took a long time to feed through into aggregate demand reducing the ability of governments to fine-tune economic activity successfully.

2. Once state expenditure was increased it proved difficult to reverse the spending. It made no sense to the electorate to leave bridges, roads, hospitals, etc. half-built, and once pensions and other welfare provisions were increased it was not politically easy to attempt to reduce them.

3. The cost of large-scale government projects had a tendency to escalate out of all proportion to original estimates once the projects had commenced (recall the experience with Concorde in the late 1960s and early 1970s and the Nimrod early-warning radar project in the mid-1980s which was eventually abandoned).

4. Taxation, including national insurance contributions, as a percentage of GDP drifted upwards in the early 1960s to the mid-1970s – on one measure from around 32 per cent to 45 per cent of GDP at market prices. In other words, governments raised taxes to finance higher public spending more often than they reduced them.

In general, government spending plans were politically sensitive and therefore could not be directed to fine-tune aggregate demand in the manner Keynesian economists recommended. (How many political parties before 1979 were elected on the basis of promising to *reduce* government expenditure, even if cuts were justified from a macroeconomic viewpoint?) From the 1960s some economists began to put forward an alternative view of government spending and taxation under the banner of *public choice theory.* Under the Keynesian approach, governments are expected to operate as objective or disinterested regulators of the economy, altering taxation and public spending in the public interest to smooth out the business cycle. But why should the politicians that direct policy and the civil servants who administer it be disinterested parties? Presumably politicians seek re-election and re-election is linked to winning public popularity by spending more, for instance, on schools and hospitals, rather than less. Similarly, civil servants are most likely to benefit directly in terms of status, promotion prospects, continued employment, size of budgets handled, and so forth, if public spending programmes grow, not if they are curtailed. Public choice theory therefore dismisses the notion of disinterested fine-tuning of demand and explains the raising of public spending and taxation in terms of politicians and government administrators pursuing their own interests rather than the public interest. This viewpoint appears to have been influential, alongside monetarism, in shaping the Conservative government's approach to state spending in the 1980s.

So far we have discussed the essence of fiscal policy from the viewpoint of its role as a demand management instrument. We turn now, however, to a more general analysis of government expenditure and taxation decisions in terms of the overall structure and significance of public sector finances and their impact upon business.

Public finance

There are three broad elements to public sector finance:

1. Expenditures at national and local levels.
2. Taxation to provide an income to government in order to finance these expenditure plans.
3. Borrowing if expenditure exceeds income.

Expenditure

Governments spend vast sums of money on our behalf (for example, in 1988–9 UK public spending totalled £185.7bn). This expenditure represents a major injection into the circular flow of income, and as such is an important source of increases in the level of national income. The injection takes place at three levels:

1. At the national level by the central government (through Whitehall departments such as health, education, defence, etc.).
2. At the local level through local authorities (borough councils and county councils).
3. Through public corporations (such as British Rail and British Coal).

All of this expenditure takes the form of both current account expenditure (such as books for schools, notepaper for government offices, etc.) and capital account expenditure (buildings, roads, etc.). In addition to current and capital account items, transfer payments are also made by central and local government, for example pensions, child and housing benefits. All of these categories of expenditure play a major role in the smooth running of an economy in terms of the provision of public and social services, job creation and redistribution of the national income across different sectors of society.

Table 5.1 gives details of UK government expenditure in the fiscal years 1978/9 and 1989/90 under major departmental headings along with details of percentage changes in real (i.e. inflation-adjusted) terms. Note that, although the Conservative government's objective when elected in 1979

Table 5.1 UK government expenditure in 1978/9 and 1989/90 and percentage changes in real terms

	General government expenditure[a,b] by function in real terms (£bn)		
	1978/9	1989/90	Percentage change
Defence	16.5	19.0	15
Industry (including energy and ECGD)[c]	4.7	3.5	−26
Employment and training	2.4	3.2	33
Motorways and trunk roads	1.2	1.6	33
Housing (net of capital receipts)	9.6	3.4	−65
Other environmental services	5.4	6.4	19
Law and order and protective services	5.5	9.2	67
Education and science	20.8	23.3	12
Health	17.2	23.2	35
Social security	37.2	49.7	34
Nationalized industries (external finance provided by govt.)	4.2	1.1	−74
Debt interest	16.3	16.6	2
Total (excluding privatization proceeds)	164.8	187.5	14

[a] 1988/9 prices.
[b] Except for defence, roads and nationalized industries, the figures include local authority expenditure.
[c] ECGD: Export Credits Guarantee Department.
Source: H.M. Treasury, *Economic Progress Report*, no. 206 (February 1990), p. 2.

was to reduce public spending, they failed to do so in the 1980s. Housing and subsidies to industry including nationalized industries, are the only main areas of spending to suffer substantial real cuts, though the figures for defence, health and education, for example, may exaggerate the real increase in budgets. The inflation rates for defence equipment, health care and teachers' salaries have risen ahead of the general inflation rate. Since the mid-1980s the government's target has not been to reduce public spending overall but, more modestly, to reduce its share of GDP. This implies that public spending must rise more slowly than private sector consumption plus investment. Table 5.2 provides details of public spending/ GDP ratios since the early 1960s. The share of public spending in total domestic output rose from the early 1960s to the mid-1970s. It then fell following stringent cuts in public spending by the Labour government in 1975/6. It rose again from the late 1970s due to more spending on defence (intended) and social security at a time of high unemployment

Table 5.2 Total UK public spending as a percentage of GDP

	Total spending as a percentage of GDP
1963/4	36.3
1969/70	40.0
1974/5	48.0
1978/9	43.3
Conservative government	
1979/80	43.5
1980/1	45.3
1981/2	46.5
1982/3	46.8
1983/4	45.8
1984/5	46.0
1985/6	44.5
1986/7	43.5
1987/8	41.3
1988/9	39.0
1989/90[a]	38.8

[a] Estimate.
Source: H.M. Treasury, Autumn Financial Statement (1989); CSO, *Economic Trends,* annual supplements.

(unintended). As the economic recessions abated, the share of public spending in output fell slowly until it reached nearly 39 per cent by the fiscal year 1989/90.

Government expenditure has important implications for the business community. Any element of government expenditure which is not spent on imported goods and services potentially raises the level of demand in the domestic economy for the goods and services produced by UK firms. This is equally true whether the expenditure takes the form of transfer payments to the household sector, subsidies or grants to the business sector itself, or direct government spending. Through the multiplier effect (reinforced by the accelerator effect) the initial increase in government spending will lead to an even greater increase in the demand for the output of the business sector, boosting aggregate demand as a whole. Balanced against this, however, government spending has to be financed.

Taxation: sources and uses

Government income comes from a variety of sources, the main one being *taxation.* Other sources, which need only a brief mention here are:

1. National insurance contributions.
2. Surpluses of public corporations.
3. Rent, interest and dividends earned by central and local government.
4. Sales of public assets (i.e. privatization proceeds).
5. Direct charges to users of government services (e.g. use of beds by private patients in NHS hospitals, prescription charges for medicines etc.).

The primary function of taxation is to raise revenue to finance government expenditure but it may also be used to influence expenditure patterns (or the general level of aggregate demand as noted above), to redistribute income and wealth, and to reflect other social and political objectives. It is also tempting to look upon taxation as an 'evil' in that it can deter companies from investing more capital when high corporate tax reduces the potential returns. High personal taxation may also deter individuals from working harder to earn more, perhaps encouraging the 'black economy' in which people work for cash and do not declare their income for tax purposes. Evidence with regard to the extent that taxation *causes* a disincentive to either work or invest is, however, not conclusive (we return to this issue in Chapter 7 in discussing the role of tax cuts as a supply-side measure to stimulate output and employment).

The primary functions of taxation may be summarized as follows:

1. To raise sufficient revenue for both central and local government to finance expenditure.
2. To redistribute wealth from the better-off to the less well-off – in the UK, for example, via income tax, capital gains tax and inheritance tax and then via transfer payments to the less well-off in society.
3. Taxes, in the form of import tariffs and duties, may be used to protect domestic industries from foreign competition (see Chapter 8 for further details).
4. Taxes may also be levied on certain products to take account of their 'social costs'; for example, tax revenue from cigarette sales helps to offset the cost to the nation arising from health care for those suffering from smoking-related diseases, while the tax itself may be an incentive to give up smoking. Likewise, tax on petrol may help to encourage economy with regard to petrol consumption and hence reduce pollution from car emissions.

Political debates concerning taxation are more or less continuous nowadays, especially around budget time each year. These debates generally reflect differing views about what is or is not a 'good' tax system and structure. Clearly, it is not possible to provide a statement of absolute truth in this matter but we can identify some general principles. In general terms, a tax system may be deemed good if it is structured such that:

1. The amount of tax to be paid is easily understood by everyone.
2. Payment is convenient (e.g. via payrolls through PAYE or via tax on expenditure, such as VAT on certain types of goods and services).
3. Collection costs are minimal compared with the amount of tax collected so that net revenues are maximized; similarly, compliance costs (costs to individuals and businesses of complying with the payment of taxes, e.g. operating the PAYE system) should be kept as low as possible.
4. Tax rates can readily be adjusted up or down to reflect changing economic (or political) circumstances.
5. Work, investment and enterprise are not discouraged because of high tax levels, otherwise economic activity and tax revenues will suffer through disincentive effects.
6. Avoidance of the tax is difficult.

These principles are generally agreed. Some economists argue, however, that a further requirement is that people should pay taxes according to their ability to pay. This is far more controversial because it may conflict with the goals of minimizing evasion and collection costs and may discourage work and enterprise. In addition, this issue has strong political undertones – consider, for example, the controversy surrounding the Community Charge (or Poll Tax) system introduced in Scotland in 1989 and in England and Wales in 1990. Critics of the tax argue that it takes insufficient account of ability to pay.

The various types of tax collected by the government may be categorized in a number of ways:

Progressive.
Regressive.
Proportional.
Direct.
Indirect.

Progressive taxes

A progressive tax is one which takes a greater proportion of people's income as their income rises. This is the type of income tax system used throughout western economies. In the UK, for example, the percentage of tax paid on additional (marginal) income was either 25 or 40 per cent in 1989/90. The UK tax structure today, however, is much less progressive than it was in the past; in 1979 when the Conservative government was elected, the top rate on unearned income (interest, rent and dividends) was 98 pence in the pound and, on earned income (pensions, wages and salaries) 83 pence in the pound. According to critics of high taxation this led to a flood of tax exiles from the UK and encouraged tax avoidance (legal means to minimize taxes paid) and in some cases outright tax evasion (illegal tax dodging).

There are several arguments which can be made both for and against progressive tax systems. Generally, progressive taxes facilitate a redistribution of wealth from the rich to the poor and counterbalance, to some extent, the regressive nature of some other taxes which bear more heavily on the less well-off (see below). In addition, progressive taxation may be more politically acceptable to society in so far as it is regarded as socially just.

At the same time, however, high and progressive taxation can act as a deterrent to investment and initiative in both the business and household sectors, while encouraging tax evasion and the identification of loopholes within the system. It can also encourage a transfer of wealth to other countries or encourage the establishment of tax havens where tax rates are low. Moreover, progressive taxation may encourage growth in public spending, especially in democracies where the majority vote is for more spending on health, education, etc., and may attempt to place the cost on the shoulders of a small, if richer, minority.

Regressive taxes

A regressive tax falls more lightly on high incomes rather than low incomes – that is, it takes proportionately more from those least able to pay. An example is the Community Charge which was introduced in England and Wales in April 1990 (and a year earlier in Scotland) as a means of financing local authority spending.

Proportional taxes

Proportional taxes take a set proportion or percentage of income. For example, UK income tax is broadly proportional up to £20,700 of taxable

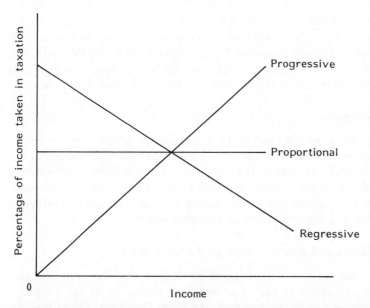

Figure 5.2 Contrasting progressive, regressive and proportional income taxes.

income in 1990/91 at a rate of 25 per cent ('broadly' because the existence of personal allowances, which are deducted before taxable income is calculated, make the tax slightly progressive). Only above this income level does the UK income tax rate become more progressive when it rises to 40 per cent.

The difference between progressive, regressive and proportional income taxes is summarized in Figure 5.2.

Direct taxes

Direct taxes are those applied *directly* to the incomes of individuals and companies and to transfers of income and wealth. Such taxes are paid to the Inland Revenue, the main categories being income tax, corporation tax, capital gains tax, inheritance tax, petroleum revenue tax on North Sea production and stamp duty (in addition, national insurance contributions for employees, though not strictly a tax, are mainly collected via the income tax PAYE system by the Inland Revenue and paid over to the Departments of Health and Social Security). Direct taxes tend to be progressive or proportional. Their main advantages, at least from the government's viewpoint, are the generally low collection costs and the fact that payment of them is usually difficult to avoid. For example, the income tax is usually around 2 per cent in the UK, due largely to the efficient PAYE system, while recent estimates put the size of the black economy in the UK at around 7 per cent of GDP (compared with well over 20 per cent in Italy). Much of the tax evasion occurs in the self-employed sector of the economy where PAYE does not operate.

Indirect taxes

Indirect taxes, which tend to be regressive in nature, are applied to expenditure and the value added to production. The main indirect tax in the UK is VAT, collected by H.M. Customs and Excise from an intermediary (for example, a shopkeeper) who then passes the tax onto the consumer in the price of goods sold. Other indirect taxes are excise duties on spirits and beers and customs duties on imported goods.

Advantages and disadvantages of direct taxation

Direct taxes are potentially fair and equitable in that they can be levied according to ability to pay (if governments choose to do so). They also act, to some degree, as automatic stabilizers (see page 84) in that the amount of tax revenue rises sharply when national income is rising, thereby increasing the leakage effect from the circular flow of income and taking some inflationary 'heat' out of the economy. Direct taxes are also less inflationary than indirect taxes since they are not levied on expenditure and therefore do not raise the price of goods and services directly.

Two disadvantages of the main direct tax, namely income tax, are often stressed: these refer to the possibility of a poverty trap and a fiscal drag effect. The combination of income tax, national insurance contributions and the possible loss of earnings-related welfare benefits as income rises, can result in an extra £1 of earned income leading to a decrease in an individual's disposable income. This represents an effective tax rate on additional income (known as the marginal rate of tax) of over 100 per cent on some low-income earners. This situation is known as the *poverty trap* and is clearly a disincentive to working. It undoubtedly also encourages activity in the black economy. In recent years, however, the raising of personal tax allowances (i.e. thresholds at which taxation begins), changes in the rates of national insurance contributions on low incomes, and reform of welfare benefits seem to have reduced the incidence of the poverty trap in the UK.

An additional problem with direct income tax arises when personal allowances and tax thresholds (at which higher marginal rates come into effect) are not increased in line with the general rate of price inflation. In this situation, income tax payments will tend to rise in real terms as people are 'dragged' into higher tax brackets or become liable to pay tax for the first time – this process is referred to as *fiscal drag* and could lead to higher wage demands as workers attempt to compensate for earnings lost in tax. In the 1980s, with the exception of one year, 1981/82, the UK government increased personal allowances and tax thresholds by at least the rate of inflation to offset fiscal drag.

Advantages and disadvantages of indirect taxation

It is argued that indirect taxes are preferable to direct taxes in that the consumer has the choice of not paying the tax (e.g. VAT) by simply not consuming the taxed good. Indirect taxes can also be levied on particular types of goods at different rates in order to encourage or discourage consumption (e.g. cigarettes). In this way, the allocation of the nation's resources may be changed from production of certain goods to other, more 'desirable' goods. On the other hand, indirect taxes may conceal the true tax burden that people face because they are hidden: the consumer may be unaware of the precise amount of tax that he or she is paying.

Indirect taxation is a flexible policy weapon in so far as the rates may be altered quickly and easily with immediate effect. This is useful from the government's standpoint in terms of the speed with which aggregate demand may be stimulated. At the same time, however, indirect taxes such

Source: Data supplied by H.M. Treasury in a budget briefing, released 20 March 1990.

Figure 5.3 Sources of UK tax revenue 1989/90.

as VAT tend to have an inflationary impact on the economy. By raising retail prices by the amount of the tax levied, there is a danger that this will tend to push up wage demands and may lead to a wage–price–wage spiral. Also, as noted above, indirect taxes tend to be regressive in nature, though a system of indirect taxes on luxury goods would be less regressive than, say, taxes on goods accepted as 'essentials' (e.g. televisions, furniture, etc.). A summary of the sources of UK tax revenue for 1989/90 is shown in Figure 5.3.

As noted earlier, government expenditure is financed largely by tax revenue. However, when total expenditure exceeds this revenue, the government, just like any firm or household, has to borrow to finance the difference. We now turn to this aspect of public sector finance which has a major role to play in the operation of fiscal policy as a demand management instrument.

Government borrowing

Deficit financing

The annual budget speech in mid-March is the occasion when the UK Chancellor of the Exchequer confirms the government's expenditure and revenue plans for the coming year. The budget represents the government's fiscal strategy or *fiscal stance*. For example, the fiscal stance at a time of a deflationary gap may be one of *deficit financing* whereby the government seeks to boost the economy by planning for a budget deficit (i.e. government expenditure is planned to exceed tax revenue). The effect of this is intended to be an expansion of aggregate demand leading to more income and employment through the multiplier effect. On the other hand, if the economy is overheating (i.e. an inflationary gap is emerging), the government could budget for a surplus of revenues over government spending in order to slow down the general level of economic activity. In this way, the budget is a major policy instrument available to a government to help it achieve particular economic objectives, for example higher employment, faster economic growth and lower inflation.

The public sector borrowing requirement (PSBR)

The amount of money which the public sector borrows during a given financial year is called the *public sector borrowing requirement* (PSBR).

The size of the PSBR is determined by a number of factors, namely:

1. The size of the budget deficit of central and local government.
2. The size of the deficit of nationalized industries and other public corporations financed by borrowing from non-government sources.
3. The amount of net lending to the private sector and overseas.
4. The public sector's receipts from the sale of financial assets and other financial transactions.
5. The public sector's receipts from the sale of real assets (e.g. the proceeds from privatization and council house sales).

When there is a negative PSBR (that is when total tax revenues exceed total public sector expenditure) there is a budget surplus which is referred to in the UK as the *public sector debt repayment* (or PSDR). A PSDR means that the government is in a position to repay some of its accumulated borrowings from previous years which make up the *national debt*.

A balanced budget

When the totals of government spending (G) and taxation (T) are the same in any year, this situation is referred to as a *balanced budget*. It is important to appreciate, however, that a balanced budget is not the same as a *neutral* budget. A budget stance is said to be neutral when the level of aggregate demand in the economy and hence economic activity is left unaltered. In contrast, comparable expenditure and tax changes within the context of a balanced budget will not have the same effects upon aggregate demand and on national income. Consider the following example.

Suppose that the government raises its expenditure (G) by £1bn, financed entirely by an increase in tax revenue (T) of £1bn leaving the overall budget balanced. Assume also that consumers spend 80 per cent of any increase in their incomes while 20 per cent is saved. That is, the marginal propensity to consume (mpc) = 0.8 and the marginal propensity to save (mps) = 0.2. Ignoring the effect of taxation, the initial injection due to an increase in G will boost aggregate demand and will eventually result in national income (Y) rising by:

$$\Delta Y = \frac{1}{mps} \Delta G = 5 \times \text{£1bn} = \text{£5bn}$$

This is as a consequence of the multiplier effect (see Chapter 4 for an explanation of the mpc, the mps and the multiplier).

At the same time, however, the increase in taxation will have caused a rise in leakages from the circular flow of income which act to reduce the effect of injections of extra demand on the level of national income. Taking account of taxation makes the net result of the rise in government spending and taxation less straightforward than our example suggests. Part of any increase in taxation may be financed by reducing the rate of *savings*. To the extent that this happens, then the increase of the leakage due to taxation will be offset by a reduction in a second leakage, savings. In other words, the *net* change in leakages is less than the change in taxation. Consequently, only that part of any increase in taxation which is financed by a reduction in consumer spending will affect the level of aggregate demand and national income. The initial impact of this will be given by 0.8 × ΔT (i.e. mpc × the change in taxation) which will have a (negative) multiplier effect on aggregate demand in general, equal to:

$$\frac{\text{mpc} \times \Delta T}{\text{mps}} = \frac{0.8 \Delta T}{0.2} = £4\text{bn}$$

Hence, the *net* result of an equivalent increase in G and T is that national income rises by (£5bn − £4bn) = £1bn. The *balanced budget multiplier* in this situation is therefore equal to 1 (i.e. $\Delta Y / \Delta G = £1\text{bn}$).

In general, allowing for savings, taxation and also imports, a balanced budget will have an expansionary effect on national income, as in our example. The impact of expenditure upon imports is reflected in the balanced budget multiplier in exactly the same way as savings.

Criticisms of fiscal policy and deficit financing

Traditional Keynesian demand management techniques place considerable emphasis on the use of the budget to influence the level of economic activity, as discussed earlier in this chapter and in the last chapter. It was conventional for governments in the post-war years to run a budget deficit financed by borrowing. From the early 1950s UK governments ran budget deficits in all but one financial year (1969/70) until 1986. After 1986 the government had sizable budget surpluses. The UK government's budgetary stance in the 1980s is set out in Figure 5.4.

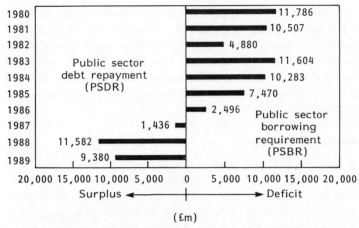

Sources: *Annual Abstract of Statistics* (London: HMSO, 1990); *Financial Statistics* (London: HMSO, February 1990).
Figure 5.4 UK budgetary stance in the 1980s.

During the 1970s, however, concern began to grow among economists about the economic effects of persistent deficit financing. This was especially true among *monetarists* (see Chapter 6). While these economists recognized the importance of fiscal policy from a budgetary viewpoint, they had a number of criticisms to make about the way in which fiscal policy measures, via the budget, were directed at controlling aggregate demand in the economy. Essentially, monetarists expressed concern regarding the effect that government deficit financing (i.e. a PSBR) had on the money supply and hence inflation. They dismissed direct management of aggregate demand and national income via fiscal policy as potentially destabilizing and indeed argued that this sort of policy had little impact upon the 'real' economy in the long-run. By the real economy they were referring to the growth in physical output, and therefore employment, as against a rise in prices which leads to a growth only in the money value of production.

In more specific terms, the monetarist criticisms of fiscal policy and deficit financing may be summarized under the following headings.

Intervention versus the free market

Keynesians and monetarists disagree fundamentally about the role of the state in managing the economy. On the one hand, monetarists tend to favour free enterprise and competition, arguing that government intervention via demand management and fiscal policy measures hampers competitive forces and discourages an enterprise culture. They also maintain that government expenditure is used as a prop for declining industries and hence fosters and perpetuates inefficient production. At the same time, high taxation to finance this expenditure, they argue, impedes the development of new growth industries. This critical view of the role of government and the use of fiscal policy can be readily associated with the approach of Mrs Thatcher's administration in the 1980s to state intervention in the economy.

Destabilizing the economy

Keynesian economists regard fiscal policy as an effective way to dampen down the economic fluctuations associated with the business cycle. Monetarists, however, argue that, far from dampening these fluctuations, fiscal policy has had the effect of destabilizing the economy by exaggerating the booms and slumps. They argue that this has largely been due to attempts by successive governments in the past to maintain aggregate demand at unsustainable high levels. This has thereby built up inflationary pressures, which have been further fed by more government spending and by the printing of 'excess' money (see Chapter 6) to ward off rising unemployment as industry became less price competitive.

Impact of deficit financing on private sector investment

Monetarists also argue that if the government borrows to finance budget deficits, this forces up rates of interest in the financial markets. While the government has the ability to pay increased interest charges, either by raising taxes or by borrowing even more funds, the same does not apply to private sector firms. Faced with higher interest rates, they may be forced to cut back on investment plans. In addition, as interest rates rise, the exchange rate is also likely to be pushed up (see Chapter 9 for a discussion of the relationship between interest rates and exchange rates). A rise in the external value of the currency will damage firms' competitive position leading to a reduction in exports – while this in turn may cause still further cut-backs in investment expenditure as well as in employment.

This phenomenon, whereby increased government expenditure financed by increased borrowing may lead to a reduction in private sector investment, is referred to by economists as *crowding out* (i.e. government borrowing crowds out private sector borrowing in the capital markets). It must be said that in the case of the UK, evidence regarding the existence of crowding out is not conclusive. Studies undertaken in the USA, however, do point to some support for this criticism of government borrowing. As world capital markets become more and more integrated and as the growth of multinational companies which can tap various capital markets continues, the relevance of crowding out is likely to diminish. It is unlikely that one government's borrowing, even when large, will have a significant impact upon the availability of worldwide capital funds for private investment.

Impact upon money supply growth

Monetarists argue that a persistent PSBR forces the government into greater borrowing from the banking sector, causing the money supply to grow much faster than the output of goods and services, leading to inflation (the process by which this takes place will be discussed in the next chapter). A common monetarist slogan to sum this up is: 'too much money chasing too few goods causes inflation'. As the money supply and inflation grow, the international competitiveness of firms declines and unemployment rises.

Monetarists, therefore, preach that governments should not try to manage aggregate demand directly but, instead, should focus their efforts on trying to create a stable economic environment in which private enterprise can flourish. They argue that this is most readily achieved by reducing state intervention, balancing the government budget from year to year, and controlling the amount of money circulating in the economy in order to diminish inflationary pressures and expectations of inflation.

Concluding remarks

In this chapter we have studied the nature of fiscal policy, trends in fiscal policy in recent years and its use as a countercyclical tool. The notion that government, by changing the levels of taxation and public expenditure, can significantly influence aggregate demand and hence the level of economic activity proved attractive in the post-war period. Up to the mid-1970s, governments in the UK pursued policies which were largely Keynesian in nature. However, the onset of stagflation (i.e. rising inflation and rising unemployment) coupled with the failure of prices and incomes policies led to a policy reappraisal. Firstly, research identified failures in operating countercyclical (i.e. stop–go) policies – in particular there seemed to be a built in 'ratchet effect' in which government spending and taxation rose but were rarely cut back, leading to what appeared to critics to be an ever-expanding state sector. Secondly, the theory that lay behind Keynesian economics, and which justified demand management by fiscal policy, was challenged by the rise of an alternative school of thought in economics, monetarism, to which we now turn.

6

Management of the economy II: Monetary policy

The essence of monetary policy

Monetary policy is generally concerned with any measures used by the government to influence the availability or price of money (i.e. the rate of interest) in an economy. In the UK, the responsibility for operating the government's monetary policy rests, through Her Majesty's Treasury, with the Bank of England. Growth in the importance of monetary policy as an instrument of macroeconomic management in recent years is explained to a large extent by the apparent failure of fiscal policy measures in the early 1970s to reduce the twin problems of inflation and unemployment – referred to as *stagflation*. As noted in the previous chapter, this failure was explained by monetarist economists in terms of excessive government spending financed by spiralling budget deficits. These deficits were not only financed through borrowing, both from the banking and non-banking sectors, but increasingly through the printing of new money. Both of these led to an increase in the money supply in excess of the amount needed to finance transactions arising from a growth in the physical output of the economy.

Monetarists argue that if the money supply is allowed to grow faster than the economy's output then households and firms will find themselves holding larger money balances than they desire to hold. This surplus of money balances will, therefore, be spent on goods and services leading to an increase in aggregate demand beyond the ability of the economy to supply. According to monetarists, this will result in a general rise in prices – an inflationary gap caused by excessive monetary growth. In addition, any upward pressure on prices will also fuel expectations of future inflation, resulting in higher wage demands and an ensuing danger of a wage–price–wage inflationary spiral. A related consequence of excessive monetary growth will then be rising unemployment as the competitiveness of firms declines and as workers price themselves out of jobs.

In the eyes of monetarists, unemployment can be brought down in the longer term only if the productive efficiency of the economy is increased and if inflationary expectations are diminished. It should be appreciated, however, that these monetarist views are not universally accepted by economists and governments. In particular, some economists (notably Keynesian economists) do not believe that controlling the growth in the money supply is necessarily the best way of bringing down inflation. Nor do they accept (as we have already seen in Chapter 5) that the only solution to unemployment is to reduce inflationary expectations and improve economic efficiency. This difference in policy prescriptions led in the 1960s and 1970s to a sharp division between economists into two schools of thought: Keynesians and monetarists. However, this distinction should not be exaggerated. Today many economists do not fit neatly into either camp, preferring to argue instead for a balance of policy measures, both monetary and fiscal, to influence economic activity.

In this chapter we set out more formally the principles of monetarism and the implications for aggregate demand and for government economic policy. We also discuss the main practical problems that have risen in the implementation of monetary policy measures in the UK in the 1980s, as well as some of the criticisms levied at monetarism. Lastly, the effects of monetary policy measures on business, particularly with regard to the effect of interest rates upon the country's exchange rate, are also examined.

Principles of monetarism

At the most general level, it is not difficult to identify why money is important in the determination of aggregate demand. If the money supply is allowed to rise it will eventually mean that, firstly, people and firms have more money in their pockets or bank accounts and, secondly, interest rates in general will tend to fall. Consequently, consumers and investors will have the potential to affect aggregate demand through their purchasing

Figure 6.1 The money transmission mechanism.

power, that is they can use these funds to buy goods and services and for investment purposes such as purchasing government bonds and stocks and shares as well as investing in land and buildings. Increased consumer and investment spending then feed through into higher demand in the economy, affecting production, employment and inflation. This process by which a rise in the money supply affects aggregate demand and in turn money GDP (i.e. GDP at current prices) – what monetarists call the *money transmission mechanism* – is summarized in Figure 6.1. A rise in aggregate demand may also have implications for the balance of payments if more imports are purchased (a discussion of this aspect of monetary growth is left until Chapter 9).

The significance of the role of money in the economy and the principles of monetarism are based on the *quantity theory of money*, which relates monetary growth to the rate of inflation. This relationship was first presented in formal terms by the American economist Irving Fisher in 1911, but the general idea that there is a link between a growth in the money supply and price rises dates back to the eighteenth century and particularly the writings of the Scottish philosopher David Hume. The quantity theory of money can be expressed in the following form:

$$MV = PT$$

where M is the supply of money in the economy, V the velocity of circulation of money around the economy, P the average price of all transactions in the economy, and T the total number of transactions in the economy in a particular time period. (Note that we previously used M to denote imports. It is, however, standard to denote the money supply by M also, and the context will clarify the meaning where necessary.)

The quantity theory is usually referred to as an identity rather than an equation because both sides of the expression are nothing more than equivalent ways of measuring economic activity: PT is a measure of the total expenditure in the economy, while MV is the total amount of money spent; both must be identical in money value. To clarify this even further, MV is the product of the amount of money available in the economy and the average number of times that this quantity of money passes around the economy as it is spent on transactions in a given time period, while PT is the value of those transactions. The stated equality must, by definition, be true although it should be appreciated that there are many measurement problems associated with its verification. For example, do we include in M only notes and coins or all forms of potential purchasing power, and how do we go about measuring the total number of transactions in the economy? The measurement of V is particularly problematic despite much research on the subject.

Monetarists have traditionally made a number of assumptions which transform the MV = PT relationship into a vehicle for predicting the likely impact of monetary growth upon inflation. In particular, they make two key assumptions:

1. The velocity of circulation of money (V) is believed to change very slowly over time and independently of changes in the money supply – therefore, it can be treated as a constant.

2. Since monetarists believe that the economy has an in-built tendency to establish an equilibrium national income at full employment, it is assumed that the total number of transactions (T) is relatively constant in the short run (in other words, that T is restricted by the productive capacity of the economy at full employment).

These two assumptions relating to the constancy of V and T have been subject to much debate and criticism by economists over the years. We return to this issue later in the chapter, but for our present purposes we need only note from these monetarist principles that if V and T are constant then prices will vary directly with the amount of money in circulation. Moreover, on the basis of empirical testing, monetarists also argue that the direction of causation is from changes in M to changes in P and conclude that 'too much money chasing too few goods causes inflation'. In other words, and in very simplistic terms, if the money supply increases by 20 per cent then this should *eventually* lead to a 20 per cent increase in prices (in practice, the relationship is not so precise because V and T do not remain constant). The time taken for an increase in M to cause a rise in P is usually estimated to be around eighteen months to two years.

In addition to the above assumptions which are necessary to create a direct link between changes in the money supply and changes in prices, there are a further three propositions to which all monetarists seem to subscribe. These are:

1. The money supply can be controlled by the authorities – this is necessary if governments are to target and control the rate of growth in the money supply to limit the growth of money GDP.

2. A competitive private sector economy automatically tends towards a 'natural' rate of unemployment and output (see Chapter 2 for an explanation of the concept of a 'natural' rate). Therefore, there will be no long-term unemployment as envisaged by Keynes unless competition in markets (including the labour market) is impeded. For this reason monetarists reject Keynesian demand management policies, believing that they create uncertainty (with regard to investment, for example), and instead tend to favour supply-side reforms (see Chapter 7) alongside sound money policies.

3. By a sound money policy monetarists mean that there should be a steady rate of growth in the money supply, corresponding to the growth in real output, in order to achieve a stable level of prices. This gives rise to 'monetary targets', discussed below.

The validity of monetarist principles, like most theories in economics, is fundamentally dependent on the underlying assumptions being shown to be correct over time, in particular the constancy of V and T. However, quite apart from this, the testing of monetarism is also fraught with practical problems, not least with regard to measuring the quantity of money in circulation.

Measuring the money supply

What is money?

In principle, anything can be classified as money. The only condition is that whatever we decide to call money must be readily accepted as a medium of exchange (that is, individuals and firms must readily accept it in return for goods and services). For example, for a short time in Germany in 1945 cigarettes were traded for goods and services, hence they acted as a crude form of money. But normally, of course, we associate money with the notes and coins in our pockets issued by governments. These pieces of paper and metal carry the authority of government and are therefore usually readily accepted by individuals and businesses as a means of payment in day-to-day transactions. This does not always hold true, however, for confidence in a government's currency may cease to exist, for example in countries where there is very high inflation or political instability.

In addition to legally issued notes and coins we could include in a definition of money other forms of purchasing power, notably deposits held in bank current accounts and building society accounts which can be accessed easily. Like notes and coins, these are *liquid assets* because they can be quickly converted into cash at little if any loss. Why include only current accounts? Money can often be withdrawn fairly quickly from savings accounts, National Savings Certificates can be redeemed and securities such as government bills and bonds can be readily sold in the stock market. These are assets which are less liquid than cash and bank current accounts but can be quickly converted into cash, usually without a major financial penalty; they are therefore sometimes referred to as *quasi-money* or *near money*. Also, a good deal of consumer expenditure today is financed by credit, i.e. hire purchase finance, credit cards, etc. It should be appreciated, therefore, that there are problems in drawing a clear line between money and quasi-money and sometimes changes in the

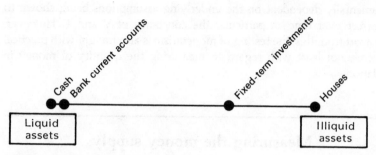

Figure 6.2 The liquidity spectrum.

financial system invalidate previous distinctions. For example, in the UK
in the 1980s, building societies became more like banks, offering accounts
almost identical to bank current accounts with cheque book facilities. For
this reason building society deposits were included in one of the
UK's official measures of money from the middle of 1987. Later, in 1989, the
Bank of England stopped reporting definitions of the money supply which
distinguished the deposits of building societies and banks.

A convenient way of illustrating the range of various measures of money
is to think of a *liquidity spectrum*. Imagine that an individual's total assets
can be classified along a scale of liquidity ranging from the most liquid to
the least liquid. Obviously the most liquid asset will be cash, while the
least liquid asset might be a person's house – especially if the owner cannot
sell the house quickly, raise equity against it easily, or does not wish to
sell it at all. Other assets can be placed between these two extremes
accordingly. For example, bank current accounts will fall close to the liquid
end of the spectrum, while a five-year fixed-term investment would lie
towards the illiquid end, as illustrated in Figure 6.2. The idea of this
personalized liquidity spectrum can be readily extended to the economy
as a whole. For official purposes, however, governments do not measure
monetary aggregates across the full range of the spectrum. Instead, in the
UK, for example, the government focuses upon a limited range of assets,
giving rise to five main money supply measures (discussed below). Before
turning to them it is important to understand the role of banks in the
creation of money and the relationship between government borrowing
(referred to in Chapter 5 as the PSBR) and the money supply.

Banks and the creation of money

Governments have the ability to increase the money supply by simply
instructing their central bank (in the UK, the Bank of England) to print

more bank notes. High street banks (commercial banks) also have the ability
to create money, however, even though in the UK they do not have the
authority to produce their own currency. They can do this by the creation
of bank deposits. Note that it is the bank deposits which create money,
not cheques as such: cheques are merely the means of transferring bank
deposits from one person to another. It is the bank deposit and not merely
the cheque which is accepted in payment for goods and services. In the
UK, commercial bank deposits are by far the most important component
of the money supply, accounting for over 90 per cent of the value
of all transactions.

There are three ways in which new bank deposits may be created:

1.   When a bank receives a cash deposit from a customer.
2.   When a bank makes a loan to a customer and this loan is then credited to
     the customer's current account with the bank.
3.   When a bank purchases a security such as a bond leading to the
     deposit of the purchase price by the seller back into the banking system.

We can illustrate the impact of the first two cases upon the ability of banks to
create credit and new deposits, and consequently, how these affect the
money supply by the following simplified example. Imagine that a bank
receives a cash deposit of £1,000 and the bank wishes to maintain a ratio
of 10 per cent cash to total deposits (either for reasons of prudence or
because it is required to do so by the authorities). It then has £900 available
for lending to willing borrowers. If the bank lends up to this total in the
form of advances, crediting these to customers' accounts, then its balance
sheet will be affected as follows:

Liabilities		*Assets*	
	£		£
Deposit (initial)	1,000	Cash reserve	1,000
Deposit (new)	900	Advances	900
	1,900		1,900

Now suppose that the borrowers spend all of these advances (£900) with
cash being drawn from the bank to meet these expenditures. Eventually
this £900 will flow back to the bank as deposits from shopkeepers, etc.
Now 90 per cent of these new deposits (£810) can be re-lent by the bank
assuming a continued cash to deposit ratio of 10 per cent (even where
there is a number of banks rather than just a single bank, provided that

they are increasing their advances at the same rate, they should receive new deposits at their branches of roughly the same amount as they lend out – therefore, the process by which deposits are created remains similar to the one in our example). Once more, these new advances (£810) will be spent and again will be redeposited. This process will continue until new deposits are negligible. It is apparent, therefore, from this simple explanation, that an initial increase in bank deposits of £1,000 cash leads to a multiple expansion of bank deposits related to the percentage cash reserve. The process, of course, cannot go on indefinitely. In general, the eventual increase in deposits following an initial deposit of cash is given by:

Increase in deposits = Initial deposit × 1/cash-deposit ratio

The fraction, 1/cash-deposit ratio, is referred to as the *bank credit multiplier* (note that this is quite distinct from the national income multiplier discussed in Chapter 4). In our example, the initial deposit of £1,000 will lead to a £10,000 increase in total deposits (£1000 × 1/0.1). It is obvious, therefore, that the extent to which the bank is able to create credit and hence its impact upon the money supply is dependent upon the cash-deposit ratio. In practice, banks may hold their assets in forms other than cash and advances, such as overnight lending to the money market and purchases of government Treasury bills (known as liquid assets because of their short-term nature) and government long-dated securities and equities (more illiquid asset forms). The holding of such assets will restrict the ability of banks to lend in the form of advances. Also, from time to time UK governments have imposed minimum requirements on banks with regard to these asset holdings in order to constrain credit expansion and hence the growth in the money supply. In the past few years, however, such restrictions have been almost entirely removed as part of a policy of deregulation in the financial sector.

Turning to the impact upon the money supply of a bank purchasing a security, there are two broad possibilities to consider. If the security is sold by the private sector and the money received is redeposited in the banking system, then we face the same situation as described above giving rise to a bank credit multiplier effect. On the other hand, if the security is sold by the government then the outcome is not so clear cut. The government can either spend the money which has been raised in this way (in which case the money will eventually find its way back into the banking system leading to a multiple expansion of credit as before) or it can retain the money as reserves. In the latter case this will result in a contraction in the bank's ability to lend and ultimately a contraction in total bank deposits and therefore the money supply. The purchase and sale of government securities in this manner to affect bank lending is referred to as *open market operations*. Indeed, the government can exercise its influence on the ability of banks to expand their lending by dealing across a wide spectrum of government securities with various dates to maturity, ranging from short-dated securities (90 day Treasury bills) to medium- and long-term government bonds. By replacing short-term government debt with longer-dated securities (a procedure known as *funding*) the authorities are able to reduce liquidity in the financial system including the banks.

Further methods by which the Bank of England can restrict credit creation by commercial banks involve special deposits and requests and directives. Special deposits were introduced in 1958 and involve the banks depositing cash at the Bank of England on which they earn interest at the Treasury bill rate but which they are unable to draw upon. These deposits are therefore illiquid assets and directly reduce the amount that the banks have available to lend. The Bank of England also has wide statutory powers to direct the activities of the banks. On occasions in the 1960s and 1970s, the Bank 'requested' or directed the banks to restrict their lending or to give priority to certain types of loan, for example loans associated with exporting. The government, through the Bank, also restricted bank credit by laying down maximum repayment periods, notably for car loans. Since 1980, the Conservative government has distanced itself from this type of direct intervention in bank credit creation for reasons discussed later.

Government borrowing and the money supply

A government can finance any excess of public expenditure over tax receipts simply by printing more money. In the UK, since the Bank of England is not a government department (technically it is a public corporation like British Rail), this would involve the Treasury borrowing from the Bank of England against the issue of new government securities (referred to as gilt-edged securities). This would amount to the printing of new money because the Treasury and the Bank of England would merely swap one 'IOU' (gilt-edged securities) for another (bank notes). The result would be a direct increase in the money supply which feeds into the economy as government departments spend. As there would be no extra production associated with this monetary expansion, it would potentially be highly inflationary. Hence, in practice, most governments eschew this method of financing their deficits and borrow from other sources than the central bank. There is a number of ways in which UK governments can borrow:

1. By issuing non-marketable debt (National Savings) which is purchased by the non-bank private sector.
2. By issuing both short- and long-term marketable debt (Treasury bills and gilt-edged securities respectively). While the former is bought by banks, most of the latter is bought by the non-bank private sector or the overseas sector.
3. By borrowing from abroad.

The first two methods are usually the most important determinants of monetary growth. An increasing PSBR will have an effect on bank deposits because the lenders to the government will use money in their bank accounts to pay for the debt securities that they purchase. It is important to distinguish the effects of public sector borrowing from both the non-bank private sector and the banking system.

If the government borrows from the non-bank private sector – i.e. the public (individuals and firms) – by issuing new securities or by means of National Savings schemes, the initial effect will be a transfer of money from the commercial banks' deposits to the government, assuming that the securities are purchased by customers using cheques drawn on their bank accounts. In the first instance, the effect of this will be to reduce the amount of money in circulation. However, the government is borrowing to spend and the money raised will eventually be paid back in one form or another to the non-bank private sector. A proportion of this money will end up as notes and coins in people's pockets, but the bulk of it will return to the banking system in the form of bank deposits by customers. Consequently, the money supply will be restored to an amount close to its original total. Therefore, in summary, when the government borrows money from the non-bank private sector there will be little net effect on the money supply, assuming that the government spends the money that it borrows which will usually be the case. If the government did not spend the money borrowed, deposits at banks would, of course, fall leading to a contraction of the money supply. When the government borrows more than it needs to finance its spending this is known as a policy of *overfunding*. Overfunding was most recently practised in the UK in the mid-1980s as the government attempted to neutralize some of the growth in the money supply taking place at that time.

On the other hand, the government may decide to borrow from the banking system. When the banks purchase government securities, as we noted above, their cash base will be reduced. Assuming once again that the money received by the government is spent, this in turn will result in a transfer of cash from the government back to individuals and firms. If this cash is then deposited in the banking system we will again perceive an increase in the total volume of deposits. In essence, the total of bank deposits will have risen and there will initially be a direct increase in the money supply equal to the amount borrowed by the government from the banking system. This initial increase will then lead to a multiple expansion of bank deposits and hence a much greater increase in the money supply via the bank credit multiplier.

In conclusion, if the government wants to control monetary growth but is unable to reduce its PSBR, it should sell debt to the non-bank private sector. Borrowing from this source does not lead to an increase in the money supply. It should be appreciated, however, that this will have implications for the level of interest rates in the economy. The government will ultimately be competing for private sector savings with banks, building societies and other financial institutions, which will tend to drive up interest rates. When the government is prepared to accept lower prices for its securities in order to raise sufficient finance in competition with the financial institutions, this will raise the rate of return on these securities. This in turn leads to higher interest rates in the economy in general: i.e. there is an inverse relationship between the price of government securities and interest rates. As interest rates are driven up, particularly if the government needs to finance an ever-increasing PSBR, there is the danger, as noted in Chapter 5, of private sector investment being squeezed: the 'crowding-out' effect.

It should be noted that reference to the money supply has so far assumed that it is defined narrowly in terms of cash and bank deposits. As we have already commented, though, money can take many forms so long as it is a readily accepted medium of exchange. We now consider official definitions in the UK.

Official definitions of the money supply in the UK

The various official definitions of the money supply in the UK are summarized in Figure 6.3. These monetary aggregates are distinguished as M0, M1, M2, etc., with extra forms of 'money' added as we progress through the series. For example, M5 is a much wider definition of the money supply than M1. The two monetary aggregates most often cited today are M0 and M4, though the government put more store on M1 than M0 in 1982 and 1983, and on M3 than M4 throughout most of the 1980s until changes in the financial markets made the M3 measure redundant. M0 is the narrowest definition of money (sometimes referred to as *narrow money* or the *monetary base*) and includes only notes and coins

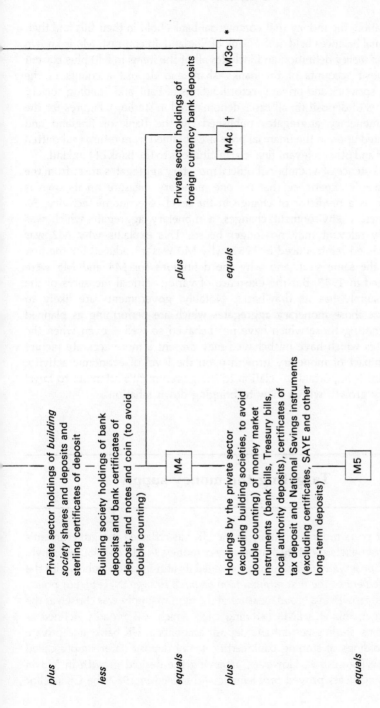

Private sector holdings of *building society* shares and deposits and sterling certificates of deposit

Building society holdings of bank deposits and bank certificates of deposit, and notes and coin (to avoid double counting)

M4

Holdings by the private sector (excluding building societies, to avoid double counting) of money market instruments (bank bills, Treasury bills, local authority deposits), certificates of tax deposit and National Savings instruments (excluding certificates, SAYE and other long-term deposits)

M5

Private sector holdings of foreign currency bank deposits

M3c *

M4c †

plus

less

equals

plus

equals

plus

equals

* Publication discontinued.
† The definition of M4c is 'anticipated' here, in advance of an official definition to be announced.

Figure 6.3 Official money supply definitions.

in circulation, the money that commercial banks hold in their tills and their operational balances held at the Bank of England. In contrast, M4 is known as a *broad money* definition and includes all of the items in M0 plus current and deposit accounts of the banks, share and deposit accounts of the building societies and private sector holdings of bank and building society certificates of deposit (in all cases denominated in sterling). Figures for the official monetary aggregates published by the Bank of England and commented upon in the financial press are obtained from returns submitted by banks and other relevant financial institutions to the Bank of England.

The existence of a number of official monetary aggregates arises from the government's experience that no one monetary measure on its own is adequate as a predictor of change in the level of economic activity. As the monetary environment changes, a monetary aggregate which was especially relevant may no longer be so. This explains why M2 was redefined and reintroduced in 1982, why M0 was introduced for the first time in the same year, and why the definitions for M4 and M5 were established in 1987. But the existence of various official measures of the money supply has its drawbacks. Notably, governments are likely to emphasize those monetary aggregates which are performing as planned while ignoring those which have not behaved so well – even when the aggregates which have misbehaved may present a more accurate picture of the impact of monetary growth upon the level of economic activity. This point is important in relation to the government's attempts to *target* monetary growth with a view to bringing down inflation.

Targeting the money supply

In recent years monetary policy in the UK has reflected the government's monetarist beliefs about the importance of money. In March 1980 the newly elected Conservative government unveiled its anti-inflation policy with the announcement of the first *medium-term financial strategy* (MTFS). For policy purposes, growth in a broad measure of the money supply was chosen as the main target; this was £M3 ('sterling M3') which was broadly defined as notes, coins, sterling current and deposit accounts at UK banks and private sector holdings of sterling bank certificates of deposit (later simply called M3 – see Figure 6.3). However, achieving the desired growth in M3 in the ensuing years proved problematic and indeed in 1987 the Chancellor

Table 6.1 Monetary targets (M3)

Target period	Target range	Outturn	Overshoot from target mid-point
	%	%	%
4/76–4/77	9–13	17.7	+6.7
4/77–4/78	9–13	16.0	+5.0
4/78–4/79	8–12	10.9	+0.9
10/78–10/79	8–12	13.3	+3.3
6/79–4/80	7–11	10.3	+1.3
6/79–10/80	7–11	17.8	+8.8
2/80–4/81	7–11	18.5	+9.5
2/81–4/82	6–10	14.5	+6.5
2/82–4/83	8–12	11.0	+1.0
2/83–4/84	7–11	9.7	+0.7
2/84–4/85	6–10	12.2	+4.2
2/85–4/86	5–9	16.6	+9.6
2/86–4/87	11–15	19.0	+6.0

Source: Financial Statement and budget reports; *Bank of England Quarterly Bulletin.*

quietly announced the end of targeting broad money in the budget of that year.

The decision to abandon the targeting of M3 came after more than a decade of increasingly unsuccessful marksmanship (see Table 6.1). Monetary targets were published initially by the Labour government from 1976, although the policy of monetary targeting reached a peak under the Conservative administration from 1979. In a speech in Autumn 1986, the governor of the Bank of England had strongly hinted that the abolition of targets for M3 was inevitable:

Only two of the past six annual target rates of growth for M3 have been achieved and, of these two, that for 1982–3 was achieved only after the target range indicated in the previous MTFS had been raised in the 1982 budget . . . . It is . . . perfectly fair to ask whether in these circumstances a broad money target continues to serve a useful purpose . . . [and whether] we would be better to dispense with monetary targetry altogether, and I shall be considering with the Chancellor whether that point has arrived in relation to broad money when we come to review the MTFS framework.

An eminent Bank of England economist, Charles Goodhart, has commented that once the monetary authorities try to control an economic statistic, which formerly may have had a close relationship to inflation, its behaviour changes so as to make it unsatisfactory (this phenomenon has been labelled Goodhart's law). The main reason for the authorities' inability to control the growth of M3 was the dramatic deregulation of the financial services sector in the 1980s and the consequent acceleration in the rate of financial innovation. The first step was taken in 1979, shortly after the new Conservative administration took office. It involved the abolition of foreign exchange controls which had existed since the Second World War. This meant that there was now nothing to prevent capital freely flowing into and out of the country. The next major landmark was the passage of two Acts of Parliament in 1986 which fostered an increasingly competitive climate in the financial markets: the Financial Services Act and the Building Societies Act. These Acts led to a flood of foreign capital and foreign financial institutions into the UK and removed many of the prudential controls under which banks and building societies, in particular, had operated. At the same time, deregulation also applied to the operation of the International Stock Exchange in London, which among other things opened up its membership to foreign financial institutions. The introduction of '24 hour' trading in stocks and shares further encouraged the inflow of foreign investment funds.

It is not difficult to appreciate why the government has generally failed to achieve its monetary targets in the light of the financial innovations which were taking place. For example, building societies are now able to offer virtually a full range of personal banking services, including cheque guarantees, personal loans, limited overdrafts, etc. Given that building society deposits were traditionally regarded as savings accounts, these changes have blurred the distinction between the M3 measure of the money stock which was formally targeted and the M4 measure which was not. At the same time, growth in the use of 'plastic money' and the introduction of facilities for electronically transferring funds (e.g. EFTPOS – electronic funds transfer at the point of sale) distorts the predictability of any relationship between the money supply and price changes.

The extent to which the financial sector responded to deregulation in the form of new financial innovations probably took the authorities by surprise. Having abolished all direct controls on lending by banks in the previous years and with the abolition of foreign exchange controls which facilitated international borrowing, the government was left only with interest rates as the policy instrument for controlling monetary growth. The Labour opposition called for a return to direct control over bank credit in the late 1980s when interest rates soared, including the use of Bank of England directives to restrain lending. But the government has continued to argue that such methods are unacceptable on philosophical and technical grounds.

On philosophical grounds the Conservative administration favours free markets and views credit controls, which limit the amounts that banks are permitted to lend, as an unwarranted intrusion into private banking. The technical argument relates to the openness of the UK money and capital markets. With the abolition of foreign exchange controls, alongside the other financial changes which produced more internationally integrated financial markets, the government argued that it would not be physically possible to restrict lending. Even in the 1960s, when the commercial banks were prevented by government from increasing their lending in line with the demand for credit, new quasi-banks such as hire purchase finance companies (some owned by the commercial banks) spread to fill the vacuum. The Conservatives argue that restrictions on credit in the UK today would merely lead to borrowing from banks abroad. In any event, they point out that credit controls are not necessarily an alternative to high interest rates. As the interest rate is the price of borrowing money, anything which restricts the supply of credit is likely to push up interest rates.

Nevertheless, interest rates alone seem to have been inadequate in recent years to restrict monetary growth sufficiently to squeeze out inflation and as such their use has been referred to as a 'blunt instrument'. There are two main reasons for this:

1. The government appears to have been unwilling to take the political risk involved in raising interest rates to the levels which were possibly necessary to arrest the growth in the money supply, especially in the mid to late-1980s. Following a sharp rise in unemployment (to over three million) associated with high interest rates in the early 1980s, the government seemed reluctant to risk any further worsening in the state of the economy.

2. Interest rate policy, especially in the period 1986–9, seems to have been focused more upon maintaining the sterling exchange rate than upon restraining the growth in the money supply (see Chapter 9).

At the same time, the government appears to have become less convinced about any direct link between M3 and inflation, and policy shifted to become more broadly based. This change of attitude is reflected in the writings of many economists in the 1980s, in that the simplistic notion of a direct link between the growth in broad money and inflation (sometimes unflatteringly referred to as *punk* monetarism) was ridiculed.

Following the demise in 1987 of M3 as the basis for monetary targeting in the UK, M0 became the only monetary aggregate for which targets were publicly announced (although the Treasury continues to monitor the growth in broad money). Instead attention switched towards maintaining the exchange rate within unpublished bands and to pursuing targets for the PSBR as a percentage of GDP. Also, although the Conservative government always recognized a link between the PSBR and the growth in the money stock, the emphasis placed upon the PSBR figures seemed to wax as the interest in money supply targets waned.

M0 has remained an official target because of its close relationship historically with movements in money GDP. Monetarists who favour targeting this aggregate argue that it provides a good barometer of the level of economic activity. For example, when M0 is rising quickly this implies that economic activity (money GDP) is also rising fast. Critics of the measure, however, question whether M0 provides a useful *leading indicator* of inflation. Also, since it is made up largely of notes and coins in circulation, it is not too surprising that it rises as money GDP increases. It is not entirely clear, however, whether the causation is from M0 to money GDP or vice versa (the problem we noted earlier with regard to the $MV = PT$ relationship). When economic activity is increasing, more notes and coins are used for transaction purposes. Perhaps, somewhat cynically, the government could be accused of favouring M0 as its principal

Source: Royal Bank of Scotland.

Figure 6.4 Money supply targeting – percentage change over twelve months (seasonally adjusted).

measure of monetary growth in the late 1980s simply because it was the one which remained within or reasonably close to its prescribed target ranges. In other words, it behaved more satisfactorily than the wider definitions of the money supply such as M3 and M4 (see Figure 6.4).

Criticisms of monetarism

Just as Keynesian economics was subjected to substantial criticism in the 1970s, so too has monetarist philosophy come under scrutiny, in terms of both its theoretical foundations and its effectiveness in achieving its desired objectives.

Monetarists' views on the importance of money are based on the quantity theory of money. In essence, this implies that there is a direct and predictable relationship between growth in the money supply and inflation. Monetarists further emphasize that, based on empirical research, the direction of this relationship is from changes in M to changes in P. This has been strongly challenged, however, and as yet there is no consensus view. Just because inflation tends to follow increases in money supply, as the monetarists' empirical results show, this does not necessarily mean that the increase in the money supply *causes* inflation.

In addition, the assumed constancy of V and T by monetarists in the quantity theory has been challenged on empirical grounds. The assumption of a constant T implies that the economy is always at full employment, but clearly this will not be the case in an economic recession. If there is substantial unemployment and the authorities choose to reflate the economy by increasing the money supply, this is likely to raise T (i.e. the volume of transactions and hence output) rather than P. Consequently, the link between changes in M and changes in P will be less predictable than argued by monetarists. Turning to the assumed constancy of V, if in practice the frequency with which each unit of money changes hands is subject to change over time, this compromises the usefulness of monetary measures in relation to counterinflationary policy. For example, in the extreme case, an increase in M could be offset totally by a decline in the speed with which money circulates in the economy (i.e. through a fall in V) so that MV and therefore PT remain unchanged. Empirically, V has changed over a number of years in the UK. Figure 6.5, for example, shows the annual percentage change in the velocity of circulation corresponding to M0 and M4 since 1983 (note that V can be calculated with respect to

Source: Financial Statistics (London: HMSO, January 1990).

Figure 6.5 Velocity of circulation of M0 and M4 – annual percentage change.

any monetary measure simply by calculating $V = PT/M$ for different definitions of M).

Apart from controversy regarding the assumptions underlying the monetarists' interpretation of the quantity theory, there is also controversy over the strength of two key linkages:

1. The link between changes in the money supply and changes in interest rates.
2. The link between changes in interest rates and aggregate demand (particularly investment) in the economy.

Monetarists believe that these linkages are strong, while their critics disagree. Monetarists argue that changes in the money supply have a significant effect on interest rates, assuming that interest rates are determined in a free market (it will be appreciated that the authorities can either control the quantity of money or the price of money but not both simultaneously. For example, interest rates cannot be raised to 50 per cent and people forced to borrow limitless amounts of money against their will). This view rests on the monetarist belief that people's willingness to hold their assets in the form of money balances is relatively *insensitive* (or *inelastic*) with respect to the rate of interest, i.e. the demand for money (M_d) is relatively unresponsive to the price of money. This view is illustrated in Figure 6.6. Again, this is an area of considerable controversy which has been subject to much empirical testing and on which no consensus view has emerged. The issue seems to be one of degree, in the sense that the

Figure 6.6 Monetarist view of the link between interest rates and changes in the money supply.

demand for money does appear to be interest inelastic at high real rates of interest (i.e. allowing for inflation in the cost of borrowing). If the M_d schedule is steep (inelastic) then any change in the money supply has a strong impact upon interest rate levels. This is illustrated by a leftward shift (reduction) or rightward shift (increase) in the money supply schedule, M_s. In the case of a reduction from M_{s_1} to M_{s_2}, interest rates will be pushed up from r_1 to r_2 (see Figure 6.6). It should be noted that this schedule is drawn for convenience as a vertical line, which suggests that the money supply is determined independently of interest rates. This may not be true in reality but it is not a crucial assumption in the debate.

Keynesian economists, on the other hand, dispute the idea that the demand for money is relatively insensitive to changes in interest rates. They argue, instead, that as interest rates vary then the demand to hold money balances will fluctuate sharply as people move their balances into and out of various interest-bearing assets. Keynesian economists identify government bonds as the most obvious alternative to holding money balances because they are risk-free and, since they can be readily traded in the stock market, liquid. Therefore, Keynesians argue that the willingness to hold assets in the form of money is relatively sensitive with respect to changes in interest rates on bonds: i.e. the demand to hold money balances is relatively interest elastic, as shown in Figure 6.7. If this view is correct

Figure 6.7 Keynesian view of the link between interest rates and changes in the money supply.

then, in contrast to the monetarist conclusion above, measures taken by authorities to change the money supply will have little effect on the rate of interest. In Figure 6.7 a reduction in the money supply from M_{s_1} to M_{s_2} has only a small impact upon the interest rate, pushing r_1 only up to r_2.

Monetarists also hold a fundamentally different view of the likely impact of interest rate changes upon aggregate demand from that held by Keynesians. As we saw in the discussion of national income determination in Chapter 4, Keynesian economists argue that aggregate demand in general, and investment expenditure in particular, are fairly insensitive to changes in interest rates. In other words, any given change in interest rates is believed to lead to a less than proportionate change in total expenditure in the economy. The reasoning behind this is that, even if people wish to hold extra money balances (cash) as interest rates fall, these balances may not necessarily be spent on extra goods and services (i.e. on additional transactions in the economy). Instead, it is argued, these balances may be held for other purposes associated with precautionary (unforeseen contingencies) and/or speculative motives (e.g. stock market dealings).

More specifically, with regard to investment expenditure, there is no doubt that changes in interest rates have some influence upon investment decisions, but Keynesian economists argue that the relationship is unlikely to be precise. The reasons for this view are:

1. Investment expenditure in the public sector is undertaken for a host of reasons – social, political and economic – which may not be affected by the interest rate level.

2. Investment expenditure plans in the private sector commonly stretch over many years and are often large scale, so short-term changes in interest rates are unlikely to be a critical factor.

3. The key determinant of investment in the private sector is the *expected* rate of return on capital (discounted to present values) relative to the cost of borrowing money (the discount factor): the volatility of expectations in general will have a major effect on investment decisions and interest rates are but one factor in determining expectations.

For these reasons Keynesians believe that even if changes in the money supply cause a significant change in interest rates, the relationship between changes in interest rates and the level of investment is unpredictable. For example, as Keynes pointed out, in an economic recession, when business expectations are depressed, reducing interest rates may not lead to more investment – he likened the use of interest rate reductions in such circumstances to 'pushing a piece of string'.

In contrast, monetarists argue that the rate of interest is a main determinant of investment decisions. The reasoning behind this view is that a fall in interest rates will make some investments profitable, which were previously unprofitable, and therefore aggregate investment should increase (and vice versa when interest rates increase). Therefore, aggregate investment in the economy is inversely related to the rate of interest. The difference between the Keynesian and monetarist views on the impact of interest rate changes upon investment is summarized in Figure 6.8 where the curves labelled I represent levels of investment at different interest rates (referred to as *marginal efficiency of investment curves*). I_1 is a Keynesian representation where investment is not particularly affected by moderate changes in interest rates. I_2 shows the monetarist position where interest rates do have a significant effect on the amount invested. Empirical evidence on aggregate investment seems to confirm that it has an inverse relationship with interest rates but that it is a fairly weak one and with varying time lags before investment responds. Therefore, as with the linkage between changes in the money supply and interest rates, the evidence on the effect of interest rate changes on investment is inconclusive.

Apart from these criticisms, monetarism has been questioned in terms of the effects that it has on an economy and on the practicality of

Figure 6.8 Link between interest rates and investment – Keynesian and monetarist views compared.

implementing the measures necessary to bring about the effects desired by monetarists. This is particularly true in the context of an economy operating with considerable excess capacity. The high interest rates that may be required to bring about stable prices in an environment of high inflation may be socially and politically unacceptable as well as economically damaging. Social and political acceptability is a particular problem facing democratically elected governments, such as the Conservative government at the start of the 1990s. Perhaps not surprisingly, some of the major success stories for monetarism in reducing inflation occurred where governments were not so vulnerable to political pressures, such as in Chile under military rule after 1973.

Moreover, it has been argued by the critics of monetarism that the economic effects of a strict monetarist strategy may be even worse than the consequences of the inflation that it seeks to remove. These suggested effects are:

1. There may be a sharp increase in unemployment as a result of deflationary monetary measures, i.e. a credit squeeze coupled with high interest rates.
2. Rising unemployment will reduce tax receipts to the government and

at the same time will put increased pressure on public expenditure and the PSBR, making control of the money supply more difficult.

3. A strict monetarist approach is likely to require a reduction in the PSBR: this brings with it a conflict between economic policy and maintaining a government's social objectives through expenditure on welfare programmes.

4. Monetarists emphasize the favourable effects of their policy recommendations over the longer term, but in the meantime the economic suffering may lead to a change in government and a change in economic strategy; thus any long-term benefits that might have accrued will never be realized.

5. A sharp rise in interest rates which are then held at a high level for some time may arrest investment and reduce economic growth. At the same time, businesses may also be hampered by the effect of high interest rates on the exchange rate.

The effects of monetary policy on business

Monetarists contend that, by pursuing a policy of strictly controlling the growth in the money supply, an economic environment will eventually be created in which enterprise and efficient firms can flourish. After the credit squeeze and recession necessary to remove inflationary pressures, firms will be left 'leaner and fitter' and therefore better able to take advantage of the available opportunities which will emerge in a post-inflationary economy. Clearly, therefore, the positive effects of monetary policy on business must be looked at from a long-term perspective – and perhaps by a government with a great deal of confidence and strong nerve.

As we have intimated on several occasions in this chapter, however, monetarist measures to reduce inflationary pressures are likely to have a number of negative effects on business, at least in the short term. Possible negative effects include the impact upon exchange rates, profits, investment and even the very survival of some firms. For example:

1. High interest rates will tend to hit exporters since high interest rates attract foreign currency into the economy causing the external value

of the currency to rise. Under certain circumstances this reduces the competitiveness of exports in foreign markets. At the same time, as the value of the currency rises, domestic producers suffer as imported goods gain a competitive price advantage. These effects follow since an appreciation in the foreign exchange rate makes exports more expensive in foreign markets and imports less expensive in the home market. There may, therefore, be unfavourable consequences for the balance of payments. Chapter 9 discusses the relationship between the exchange rate and the balance of payments.

2. High interest rates coupled with a high exchange rate will tend to decrease aggregate demand for domestically produced goods. This is, therefore, likely to lead to a squeeze on profits with a consequent unplanned increase in stocks of unsold goods. To finance the costs of holding these stocks, firms may have have little choice but to borrow even more money despite high interest rates (this is sometimes referred to as 'distress borrowing').

3. Ultimately, firms may not be able to survive in a high interest rate and high exchange rate environment. The closure of firms has obvious implications for unemployment, investment and the future productive capacity of the economy. Some firms that shut down will be those that are the least efficient and creditworthy. At the same time, however, otherwise healthy firms may be caught out by a credit squeeze which leads to cash flow difficulties. Firms which have committed themselves to massive investment programmes and those which are heavily dependent upon exporting are especially vulnerable to rising interest rates.

Many of the scenarios described above have been precisely those that have faced the business community in the 1980s under the Conservative government. For example, reputedly 20 per cent of UK manufacturing capacity was lost between 1979 and 1982. At the time of an appreciating exchange rate, the government adopted a high interest rate policy to reduce monetary growth. During that period, the country witnessed a record number of bankruptcies but subsequently the efficiency and competitiveness of British industry improved. Therefore, it is possible for critics of government policy to attack the Conservative government for destroying the UK's industrial base during its monetarist experiment of the early 1980s, while at the same time the government's sympathizers can point to evidence supporting the 'leaner but fitter' view today.

Concluding remarks

From the late 1970s, government policy switched away from Keynesian-style demand management towards emphasis on control of the money supply. The switch was especially noticeable in the UK, where previous governments were mostly wedded to the Keynesian doctrine, but it was also evident in many other countries too. This change in stance on economic policy arose because of disillusionment with Keynesian economics during the stagflation of the 1970s. More recently, monetarism in turn has been criticized.

In part, criticism has centred upon the theoretical foundations of monetarist beliefs. In particular, whether there is a causal relationship between changes in the money stock and changes in price levels which can be predicted. In addition, monetarist policies have proved difficult to implement effectively. Finding a measure of the money supply which captures the effect of monetary changes on inflation has proved tricky, especially one which can be used with confidence and which can define desirable money supply targets which can actually be met. With the abolition of exchange controls and financial deregulation in the UK, the Conservative government felt it necessary to fall back upon manipulating interest rates to restrain the rise of credit in the economy. But high interest rates in turn have proved difficult to sustain over long periods for political and economic reasons. Moreover, from the mid-1980s to 1989 interest rates appeared to be set more with a view to influencing the level of the exchange rate rather than with a view to constraining the growth in the money stock. It would merely be coincidental if the interest rate needed to maintain a particular exchange rate was also the right one to achieve the money supply target. Not surprisingly, interest rate policy in this context has been described as a 'blunt instrument'.

7

Supply-side economics

The essence of supply-side economics

In the previous two chapters we considered the nature of Keynesian and monetarist economics. Both are concerned with macroeconomic policies to influence the level of *aggregate demand* in the economy – Keynesian economics primarily through fiscal measures and monetarism through controlling the growth in the money supply and interest rates. In recent years, however, some economists have switched their attention to the *microeconomic* factors which determine *aggregate supply*. They argue that the key to reducing unemployment and inflation lies in improving the ability of the economy to supply goods and services efficiently. In other words, unemployment will fall permanently only if British goods are competitive in world markets. Similarly, the reverse side of the 'excess aggregate demand' cause of inflation is an insufficient aggregate supply of goods and services to meet the current demand. In practice, most supply-side economists also favour a sound money policy to keep down inflation and to provide a conducive economic environment for employment and production. Therefore, while supply-side economics is distinct from monetarism in the sense that it is possible to support monetarist principles without favouring supply-side reforms (and vice versa), many monetarists may also be labelled as 'supply-siders'.

Supply-side economics as it is discussed in this chapter is fairly new, having emerged as a distinct area of policy analysis in the mid-1970s, but

130

the idea that government economic policy should be concerned with supply as well as demand is not new. Throughout the post-war period successive governments in the UK, the USA, France, West Germany, Japan and elsewhere intervened from time to time with initiatives aimed at increasing production. During this period these initiatives were grouped together under the title of *industrial policy*. Industrial policy measures were introduced to nationalize industry, raise investment, increase the supply of skilled labour, rationalize production, redistribute industry geographically, and to increase exports. In France (and with less success in the UK in the 1960s) economic activity was occasionally planned from the centre through the use of what were called *national plans*. These plans set down targets for the growth in production, exports, etc. over the following years. Also, the Ministry for International Trade and Industry (MITI) in Japan has been credited with aiding the expansion of Japanese industry since the 1950s by identifying potential markets and assisting investment programmes.

Modern supply-side economics is distinct from earlier industrial policy, however, because the emphasis is on establishing an economic environment conducive to private enterprise, rather than state planning and investment subsidies. Supply-side measures are thus aimed at creating an economic environment in which there is more incentive for individuals to work and save and for firms to invest, produce and employ. At the same time, supply-side economists tend to assume that aggregate demand will usually or always be sufficient to buy whatever the economy produces (in the sense that 'supply creates its own demand'). Therefore, the role of government should not be to 'plan' industry and demand, but to liberalize markets, reduce taxes and public spending and free-up the labour market.

A primary objective of supply-side policies is the creation of the necessary economic conditions to achieve fast economic growth, full employment and low inflation. In this chapter we look in particular at the policies which have been pursued to that end by the Conservative government since 1979, namely:

1. Changes in trade union laws to restrict the power of trade unions.
2. The reduction of taxation and the creation of greater incentives to work and invest.
3. The programme of privatization.

We begin by considering the economic theory which underlies supply-side economics.

The principles of supply-side economics

In essence, supply-side economics is concerned with increasing aggregate supply so that more demand can be accommodated without inflation. An economy's aggregate supply consists of the various amounts of total real output that producers are able and willing to produce at various price levels. Therefore, an economy's aggregate supply curve reflects the relationship between the volume of production in the economy at different price levels. In principle, the aggregate supply curve can be horizontal, upward sloping or vertical, depending upon the precise relationship between rising prices and output (since producers are most unlikely to supply more at lower prices, however, the supply curve will presumably not be negatively sloped). These possible shapes are illustrated in Figure 7.1

There is no real consensus among economists, however, about which type of aggregate supply curve is most likely. A horizontal supply curve such as AS_1 suggests that supply will increase without a rise in the price level in the economy – which implies that output can rise without unit (average) costs rising. In other words, more workers can be attracted into

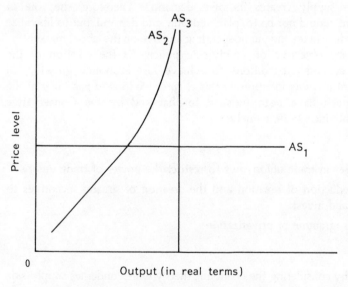

Figure 7.1 Aggregate supply schedules (AS).

employment without offering higher real wages, more capital can be obtained for investment without an increase in interest rates, and an increase in the demand for raw materials and components does not cause their unit price to rise. This situation is most likely to be found where there is substantial unemployment of resources..

In contrast, an upward sloping aggregate supply curve such as AS_2 implies that higher units of output are associated with a higher price level. Higher prices may be necessary to induce firms to produce more. Also, increased output means more demand for factors of production such as labour and capital which may raise their unit price and therefore unit production costs. As the economy gets closer to Keynesian full employment (or, from a monetarist perspective, the natural rate of unemployment – see Chapter 2) so prices are driven higher for each proportionate increase in output.

Lastly, a vertical aggregate supply curve such as AS_3 means that the volume of (real) output cannot rise. Keynesians associate the vertical aggregate supply curve only with a fully employed economy (see Chapter 5), but some monetarists argue that, since workers appreciate the meaning of purchasing power, a mere increase in *money* wages does not lead to more employment and therefore output will not rise. For example, if workers are offered £10 per week more to attract them into employment or to work overtime, but this is completely offset by rising prices, then no more labour will be supplied since (real) wages will not have changed. Similarly, in so far as firms increase output in response to the lure of higher real profits, a doubling of profits alongside a doubling of prices will have no effect on their decision to supply (this 'rational' behaviour is in keeping with a branch of monetarist philosophy couched within *rational expectations theory*). Consequently, output is unaffected by (i.e. is independent of) the price level. At best, there may be only a temporary rise in output when prices rise until such time as workers and firms realize that the increases in wages and profits do not amount to real increases. In other words, until expectations about further inflation adapt to the actual price rise.

The precise nature of the aggregate supply curve is important in appraising the value of Keynesian demand management techniques for the following reason. If the aggregate supply curve is horizontal, an increase in aggregate demand resulting from an injection of government spending or a reduction in taxation will lead to more output and therefore more employment without the emergence of inflation. This is shown by the shift in aggregate demand from AD_1 to AD_2 in Figure 7.2 with the price level remaining at P_1 but output rising from Y_1 to Y_2. Even where the aggregate supply curve is upward sloping, although more demand produces some rise in prices (inflation), output and employment will still increase.

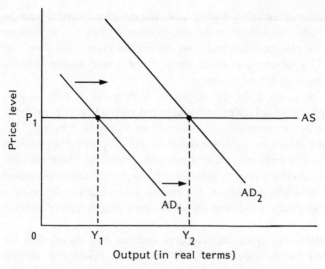

Figure 7.2 Horizontal aggregate supply schedule.

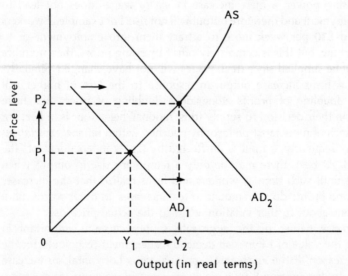

Figure 7.3 Upward sloping aggregate supply schedule.

In Figure 7.3 this is shown as an increase in aggregate demand from AD_1 to AD_2 with prices rising from P_1 to P_2 and output from Y_1 to Y_2.

Both of these possibilities, therefore, imply that Keynesian demand management techniques can boost production and employment in certain

Figure 7.4 Vertical aggregate supply schedule.

circumstances. Where, however, the aggregate supply curve is vertical, more aggregate demand merely spills over into inflation with no beneficial effects on production and unemployment since supply is fixed. This is shown in Figure 7.4 as a rise in aggregate demand from AD_1 to AD_2 leading to a corresponding rise in prices from P_1 to P_2 with output remaining at Y. Therefore, in this situation Keynesian techniques are simply inflationary and do not stimulate employment. In which case, if aggregate supply does not respond to price rises, as some economists believe, how can production and employment be increased?

According to supply-side economists, the solution lies in measures which will shift the aggregate supply curve to the right (e.g. from Y_1 to Y_2) as in Figure 7.5 (this is equivalent to shifting the production possibility curve outwards in Figure 1.2, meaning that there is potentially more of all goods and services available). This can be achieved by either (or both) of the following:

1. Increasing the availability of economic resources, i.e. more labour, capital or natural resources.
2. Changes in technology and other methods of increasing the productive efficiency with which the available economic resources are used in the economy.

Figure 7.5 Shifting the aggregate supply schedule.

Since the availability of economic resources changes slowly over time, for example as the population rises, and few changes in technology produce immediate and dramatic effects on output, it follows that shifting the aggregate supply curve to the right is a slow and continuous process. Supply-side economists argue, however, that governments can take measures to encourage the more efficient use of the existing resources and to encourage investment and technological change over the longer term.

In Figure 7.5, the aggregate supply curve is assumed vertical, though the existence of an upward sloping curve would not substantially alter the following argument. The effect of supply-side policies is to shift the curve from AS_1 to AS_2. If aggregate demand remained unchanged (AD_1), the result would be a rise in real output (from Y_1 to Y_2) alongside a fall in the price level (to below P_1). In practice, however, the purpose of shifting the aggregate supply curve is to permit aggregate demand to rise without inflation. This is illustrated by the rise in aggregate demand from AD_1 to AD_2. Note that real output has risen, from Y_1 to Y_2, but that prices have stayed constant at P_1. If aggregate demand was permitted to rise faster than aggregate supply, to AD_3, then prices would rise to P_2 but by much less than if aggregate supply had remained fixed at AS_1 (i.e. P_3).

Increasing aggregate supply, therefore, permits a higher level of demand and economic activity while suppressing inflation. This helps to explain why the study of supply-side economics has become so popular in the 1980s. Supply-side policies, especially when combined with a 'sound' monetary policy, appear to offer a means of tackling both inflation and low economic growth (and, consequently, rising unemployment), i.e. the problem of stagflation. Having studied the theory which lies behind supply-side economics, we now consider the specific supply-side measures adopted by the Conservative government in the UK in the 1980s.

Supply-side economics in practice

Since its election in 1979 the Conservative government has largely shunned the aggregate demand management policies of previous governments in favour of supply-side policies which encourage private enterprise. This development amounts to a profound shift in macroeconomic policy and has been mirrored by similar policy changes in other countries.

The Conservative government has introduced a large number of supply-side measures aimed at improving the performance of the economy by encouraging private investment. They can be grouped into three categories.

1. *Improving the flexibility of the labour market* through trade union reforms, education and training initiatives (e.g. the national curriculum and the Youth Training Scheme), housing reforms to increase the geographical mobility of labour (such as the sale of council houses to their tenants and reform of the Rent Act), social security changes and alterations to employment protection legislation, and by reducing the scope and powers of wages councils to set minimum wages.

2. *Improving economic incentives* by reducing taxation on companies and individuals to create incentives to save, invest and work.

3. *Deregulation and privatization* of public services (e.g. bus transport) and publicly-owned industries (e.g. telecommunications, gas, water and electricity). One intended side-effect of this programme has been the introduction of wider share ownership in the UK, which the government believes is important in maintaining public support for private investment and profit-making.

Improving the flexibility of the labour market

In a highly competitive labour market, wages inevitably find their free market level. This is where the demand for labour by firms equals the supply of people willing to work at a given wage rate. Once all of those wanting work at the going wage rates are employed then there is no involuntary unemployment (though some people may remain unemployed as they hold out for jobs offering higher wages). The Conservative government in the 1980s has, therefore, adopted a number of policies aimed at reducing involuntary unemployment by making the labour market more competitive or 'flexible'. Convinced that trade unions destroy jobs (by raising wages above the levels employers can afford if they are to remain competitive in world markets), the government has introduced a series of employment and trade union legislation to curb union power, namely:

1. Employment Act, 1980. This Act restricted 'secondary' industrial action (sympathy strikes) and made picketing away from the strikers' own workplace unlawful. It also limited employees' unfair dismissal rights, restricted the enforceability of closed shop agreements and repealed certain union recognition and arbitration machinery provisions.

2. Employment Act, 1982. This legislation made unions liable for damages for unlawful industrial action, narrowed the statutory definition of a trade dispute, and further restricted the enforcement of the union closed shop.

3. Trade Union Act, 1984. This statute made industrial action unlawful without a prior strike ballot and required union executives to be elected by five-yearly secret ballots.

4. Employment Act, 1988. This legislation established a Commissioner for the Rights of Trade Union Members, to assist union members with grievances to take legal action against their unions. It also required union postal ballots and prohibited both dismissal for non-union membership, and the disciplining by unions of members who refused to take part in an industrial action.

5. Employment Act, 1989. This Act limited rights for time off work for union duties and repealed certain laws regulating the work of young people. It also removed the legal requirement for small firms to provide written statements relating to disciplinary procedures.

6. Employment Bill, 1990. This Bill, before Parliament at the time of writing, abolishes the closed shop and removes legal immunity for

what are known as wildcat or unofficial strikes, i.e. strikes which do not have official union backing.

This legislation, along with high unemployment levels throughout most of the 1980s, has reduced the number of strikes in British industry, as intended by the government (see the discussion on union membership and industrial disputes in Chapter 2). In support of its policy, the government has pointed to studies which link unions with unemployment. For example, research by Professor Patrick Minford at Liverpool University suggests that the increase in trade union militancy from the early 1960s was a direct cause of higher unemployment by pricing labour out of employment. He estimates that unions push up real wages by as much as 12 to 15 per cent above their free market levels, leading to between 400,000 and 800,000 fewer jobs. Another study by Professors Layard and Nickell of the London School of Economics, published in 1985, estimated that around 23 per cent of the rise in unemployment between 1956 and 1983 was caused by the actions of trade unions.

Although it is difficult to lay the blame for the doubling of unemployment in the early 1980s at the door of the unions, 'taming the unions' has nevertheless remained a key component of the government's supply-side policies. According to the government, 'real wages un the UK have not been sufficiently responsive to labour market conditions and have risen too fast' (H.M. Treasury, *Economic Progress Report*, October 1987). The government clearly sees the unions as being one important cause of this lack of wage responsiveness, but another factor they identified was the structure of unemployment and social security benefits which evolved in the post-war period.

The extent to which unemployment benefits and other welfare payments create inflexibility in the labour market is controversial. No doubt, overgenerous payments will dull incentives among the unemployed to seek jobs. A high *replacement ratio* (the ratio of income received out of work to income received in work) will have a marked disincentive effect leading to what has been termed an *unemployment trap*. It is far from clear, however, that UK benefits are anywhere near this level. Professor Minford has been a leading advocate of the view that welfare benefits in the UK, coupled with high taxation on low incomes, have been a major disincentive to the unemployed finding work. But in 1982, the Department of Health and Social Security calculated that only around 3 per cent of the unemployed had a higher income out of work than in work, while 40 per cent had state benefits equivalent to under one-half of their in-work incomes.

Such estimates may, however, underestimate the disincentive effects of the welfare state and, in the 1980s, the UK government has attempted to make the trade-off between the dole and work less favourable to remaining unemployed. Particular measures have included indexing social security benefits to retail prices rather than earnings (earnings have grown much more quickly than prices in the 1980s), reforms in social security, and making the obtaining of benefits more difficult especially for school leavers. In addition, one of the earliest actions of the government was to subject unemployment benefits to income tax and to scrap the earnings related supplement, which provided additional unemployment benefit based on the previous level of earnings at work. These policy initiatives have helped relieve the unemployment trap so that today it is probably a problem only for a small minority of the unemployed.

Improving economic incentives

In addition to reforming welfare payments, the government has attempted to increase flexibility in the labour market by reducing the burden of taxation in the UK so as to make working more worthwhile. The policy of reducing taxes is also intended to act as a spur to investment and private enterprise. A main claim of supply-side economists is that high tax rates have created major disincentives to work, save and invest. This was echoed in the Chancellor of the Exchequer's March 1986 budget speech:

> Reductions in taxation motivate new business and improve incentives at work. They are the principal engine of the enterprise culture, on which our future prosperity and employment opportunities depend.

Between 1979 and 1989 the following major tax changes were introduced:

1. Reduction in the marginal rate of income tax on high incomes from 83 per cent on earned income and a penal 98 per cent on unearned income (e.g. interest and dividends) to a uniform rate of 40 per cent.

2. Reduction in the basic rate of income tax (the maximum rate paid by around 90 per cent of income tax payers) from 33 to 25 per cent.

3. Reduction in the rates of corporation tax on company profits from 40 and 52 per cent, depending upon the level of profits earned, to 25 and 35 per cent respectively.

4. Raising income tax thresholds to take more people out of tax, thereby reducing the extent of *fiscal drag* (see Chapter 5 for an explanation of fiscal drag).

5. Major technical changes to tax legislation aimed at alleviating the impact of capital gains tax and the taxation of lifetime capital transfers.

6. Tax exemptions and other incentives for investment in plant and buildings, new companies and financial securities (e.g. enterprise zones, the Business Expansion Scheme, share options, personal equity plans, etc.).

The idea that there is a significant relationship between tax rates and the willingness to work was popularized by the *Laffer curve*, reputedly conceived on the back of a restaurant table napkin by the Californian economist Professor Arthur Laffer. The basis of this concept is the belief that there is an optimal tax rate which will maximize government revenue. When the tax rate is zero there is, of course, no tax revenue. Equally, if the tax rate was set at 100 per cent, presumably tax revenue would also be zero since there would be no incentive to work or invest at all and, hence, there would be no income to tax. It follows, therefore, that somewhere between these two extreme rates there must be a tax rate which maximizes tax revenue. Although the precise shape of the Laffer curve is not entirely clear, it is conventional to draw it with a smooth slope and with one peak as in the right-hand side of Figure 7.6.

As the tax rate is increased from zero to T_1, government tax revenues rise as shown by the Laffer curve TT. Beyond T_1, however, raising tax rates is counterproductive. The disincentive effects of high taxation reduce the tax base (e.g. hours worked) so that, although the amount out of each pound earned taken in tax rises, the number of pounds earned falls more quickly and therefore less tax is recovered. In other words, if the current tax rate is above T_1, it would pay government to *reduce* the rate as tax revenues would actually rise.

Turning to the left-hand side of the diagram, the curve GG marks out the rate of growth in GDP (gross domestic product) per annum at different tax rates. Once again a single peak is assumed at G_1. Below G_1 a rise in the tax rate is associated with higher economic growth. The provision of certain public services financed from taxes, for example roads, defence and law and order, are conducive to private investment. Without them there would be insufficient security to produce and inadequate communications to distribute products. Beyond G_1, however, taxation and the related public spending are associated with a lower growth rate. Note that there appears to be no reason why G_1 and T_1 should be at the *same* tax rate. In other

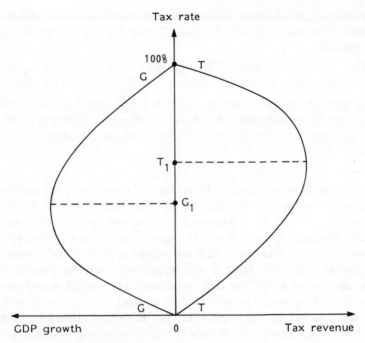

Figure 7.6 The Laffer curve.

words, the rate of tax which maximizes tax revenues to government may not be the same as that which maximizes economic growth. In Figure 7.6, G_1 is below T_1 suggesting that the tax rate which maximizes the growth in GDP is less than that which provides the largest government revenue. In this case government has a choice to make between maximizing its own income and maximizing economic growth.

On the basis of this logic, Professor Michael Beenstock in 1979 predicted that by reducing the tax/GDP ratio in the UK from 40 to 35 per cent, coupled with sharp reductions in top marginal tax rates, GDP would increase by 15 per cent. This study, however, was subsequently sharply criticized on the grounds that there was no clear evidence that reducing tax rates would necessarily cause people to work harder and produce more. In a later study for the Treasury on the impact of tax cuts upon the labour supply, Professor C.V. Brown of Stirling University concluded that: 'the changes in predicted hours are very largely the effect of the change in the level of demand constraints. Little of the change in predicted hours is the result of changes in taxation.'[1] This suggests that tax cuts are likely to have a more important effect on aggregate demand, as Keynesians would predict (see Chapter 4), than on aggregate supply.

The Laffer curve is an interesting concept and useful in so far as it draws attention to the possibility that reducing tax rates might actually benefit government revenues, while at the same time boosting economic growth. It is, however, difficult to know at any given time whether a country has tax rates which put it above or below the peaks of the growth rate and tax revenue curves. Without this knowledge we cannot say what effect cutting (or increasing) tax rates will have on the level of economic activity or government income.

Some economists are sceptical of the idea that cutting tax rates really does lead to an appreciable gain in economic growth, while others are of the view that reducing taxes may not require cuts in public spending because tax revenues actually rise. In the USA and the UK in the 1980s reductions in tax rates were indeed associated with both a rise in economic growth and more government tax receipts. The causation, however, is not clear. Economists who support tax cuts point to this experience as proof of the Laffer effect. Others, however, point out that faster economic growth *produces* higher incomes, which then generate higher tax receipts, and that it is not clear that the tax rate cuts are responsible for the higher growth rate.

In assessing the likely consequences of tax changes, economists distinguish between what are called *income* and *substitution effects*. In terms of income tax, the income effect depends upon the *average rate of tax* (art), which is equal to the tax paid (T) divided by the *tax base*, i.e. income (Y). Thus,

$$art = T/Y$$

The substitution effect, by contrast, is associated with the *marginal rate of tax* (mrt) which is equal to the change in tax paid (ΔT) divided by the change in income (ΔY). That is,

$$mrt = \Delta T/\Delta Y$$

When deciding to increase hours of work or work effort, individuals are concerned with small or marginal changes in working. Therefore, it is the *mrt* rather than the *art* which matters since this tells us what percentage of the extra income earned goes in tax. This also applies to a reduction in employment where the *mrt* determines the net of tax income forgone by not working. This means, for example, that a cut in income tax rates creates a greater incentive to work by increasing the marginal benefit of work (in terms of after-tax income), compared with the other options of leisure time or unemployment. In contrast, a cut in the income tax rate provides a disincentive to work because the amount of work needed to produce a given after-tax income is reduced. If people discover that, after the tax rate reduction they can achieve their former income with less work than previously, they may decide to work fewer hours and take more leisure. Therefore, only if the substitution effect of a tax rate dominates the income effect will there be a net incentive to increase work effort.

Apart from identifying the existence of substitution and income effects of tax rate changes, it is difficult to deduce what overall effect a tax change will have on the incentive to work and by similar logic, incentives to invest and save. Therefore, as in the case of the Laffer curve, we are able to conceptualize the effect of tax changes, but they do not take us much further forward in deciding in a specific case, such as the UK in the 1990s, whether reductions in taxation must necessarily increase economic activity. Neither theory nor empirical evidence based upon studies of the effect of taxation on work, investment and savings in the UK, provide strong grounds for believing that tax changes will lead to an appreciable improvement in economic performance. At the same time, there is equally no reason to become complacent about the effects of taxation on the economy. Presumably the logic behind the Laffer curve holds and at *some* tax rate economic growth suffers. The unanswered question is whether the UK economy prior to 1979 had tax rates which damaged the economy and, therefore, whether the reductions introduced in the 1980s have improved incentives to work, save and invest resulting in higher economic growth.

Deregulation and privatization

A third major strand of the government's supply-side reforms involves measures to make markets work better by removing barriers to competition introduced by the state. Like many economists, the government believes that competition is the key to higher productive efficiency, wider consumer choice and lower prices and therefore that monopolies, particularly public sector monopolies protected by statute, should be dissolved or at least controlled. There are two main parts to this programme: one concerns introducing competition to provide services supplied previously by public sector monopolies, the other involves the transfer of state-owned assets to the private sector. Both parts often go under the title of *privatization*, but here we shall use the term deregulation to describe introducing more competition and retain the term privatization exclusively to describe the sale of state-owned assets. A related policy involves introducing more competition in the private sector through reforming monopolies and wages legislation and removing restrictive trading practices in, for example, the stock market (such as the October 1986 'Big Bang' in the UK which, among other things, opened up membership of the London Stock Exchange to foreign-owned institutions), legal services and the supply of spectacles by opticians. This latter policy is not considered further here, however. Instead, we concentrate upon deregulation and privatization affecting public sector monopolies as these have attracted most public attention.

The government has disappointed some economists by what they see as its failure to deregulate more markets in which public sector or former public sector monopolies operate. The main initiatives have involved opening up the supply of telecommunications equipment to private firms and deregulating express coaching and local (stage) bus transport. Previously all telecommunications equipment such as telephone receivers were supplied by British Telecom (publicly owned until November 1984). In 1981, however, the government made it possible for consumers to buy and connect up to the British Telecom network equipment from competitive suppliers. Also, a new telecommunications system operator was licensed to compete with British Telecom, Mercury Communications. Turning to coach and bus transport, previously licences to operate routes were difficult to obtain as the licensing authorities seemed keener to preserve the services of existing operators than to encourage new ones. In 1980, however, express coaching and in 1986 local bus transport were opened up to competition. Although the public sector operators continue to dominate services, there is evidence that competition has produced the expected results, especially in terms of reducing prices. This was especially noticeable in the early 1980s for express coaching when fares were cut dramatically and new facilities such as video and hostess services were introduced to win over customers.

Another area in which more competition has been introduced involves central and local government and the National Health Service (NHS). Here, the government has required departments and hospitals to put out numerous services, formerly operated by public departments, to competitive tender. To retain the work, in-house units have had to slash costs, trim overmanning and abolish entrenched restrictive working practices. In local government this was given a further impetus by the Local Government Act, 1988, which made it mandatory for all local authorities to contract competitively for the following services: refuse collection, building cleaning, catering, ground maintenance, repair and maintenance of vehicles and sport and leisure management. A number of academic studies suggest potential savings for taxpayers from competitive tendering in the public sector of around 20 to 25 per cent.

A desire to raise the efficiency with which goods and services are delivered has also driven the government's privatization programme, though the widening of share ownership and contributions to the financing of government spending through receipts from asset sales have been further considerations. In the main, the government has justified privatization by pointing to higher efficiency in the private sector. To raise efficiency, by the middle of 1989 sixty-four firms had been privatized with total assets exceeding £26bn. Later in that year the water industry was privatized and plans for the sale of the electricity industry in the early 1990s are well advanced.

As in the case of the disincentive effects of taxation and welfare benefits, the policy of privatization is supported more by rhetoric than hard evidence. To date, the record of the privatized industries is mixed, although it has to be recognized that privatization is still young and that it is probably too soon to draw conclusions. The management/worker buy-out of the National Freight Consortium in 1982 appears to have been an enormous success. When shares in the company were finally floated on the stock market in 1989 they had appreciated in value to such an extent that the average worker's investment of £600 in 1982 had grown to a staggering £44,000. In contrast, however, the profitability records since privatization of Britoil, British Airways, Jaguar Cars and Rolls-Royce, for example, have been much less impressive. A recent study of twelve privatized firms concluded:

> The overall picture to emerge ... is one of substantial change. Output and profits have grown, margins have increased, employment has declined. But the relationship of these changes to the fact of privatization is not immediately apparent from the data. The privatized industries have tended to be faster growing and more profitable, but it seems that the causation runs from growth and profitability to privatization, rather than the other way around.[2]

Some studies of public and private enterprises in other countries have found that competition is the key to higher efficiency. But if this is so, what does privatization achieve? Firms such as Jaguar and National Freight already operated in competitive markets before they were privatized. Other privatized firms such as British Telecom, British Gas and the water authorities have retained most, if not all, of their monopoly powers. Also, the privatized monopolies now face an elaborate system of licensing with price controls and regulatory offices (e.g. the Office of Telecommunications, Oftel) which have been established to protect the consumer. Such regulation may reduce incentives to be efficient. For example, a regulated company might believe that higher profits coming from more efficiency will spark off an enquiry by the regulator into the company's pricing policy. In which case, it may decide not to pursue higher efficiency.

The government's privatization programme is criticized for paying too much attention to selling off state assets and too little to the state of competition after privatization. Therefore, it appears that, while the government's policy of deregulation may well bring major gains in efficiency, it is more difficult to believe that simply selling state assets will have similar benefits. The management of state enterprises has welcomed the transfer of their industries to the private sector to remove the dead-hand of government bureaucracy and to break free from Treasury control over borrowing for investment purposes (the so-called *external financing limits*). But the extent to which this managerial freedom will translate into long-term gains to private consumers rather than higher managerial salaries and profits for private shareholders remains unclear.

Concluding remarks

Reductions in taxation, reform of labour relations and privatization (including deregulation) have been pursued as part of a concerted policy to improve the performance of the British economy. These programmes, plus the other supply-side measures outlined at the start of this chapter, are the government's answer to the argument that the British economy was overtaxed, plagued by strikes and languishing under state bureaucracy in the 1970s. In so far as these claims are true, then the government's reforms should lead to improved economic performance. As we saw in Chapter 2, there is some evidence that productivity and economic growth have responded, though it is not as incontrovertible as government ministers sometimes claim. It should be appreciated that tax cuts may not necessarily lead to more work effort or enterprise; that the fall in the number of days lost through strikes has partly resulted from high unemployment and may rise again if full employment returns; and that privatization without more competition may not lead to higher efficiency.

In Chapter 2 we reviewed the failure of the British economy to perform as well as its major competitors on a number of accounts, but especially in terms of economic growth and productivity. There is clearly, therefore, scope to improve the efficiency and performance of the British economy: in other words, there is a strong case for improving the supply-side of the British economy. More controversial is whether the government's free market approach is the answer. The Labour Party and a number of economists would prefer to see a return to the more interventionist policies of the 1960s and 1970s implying more government involvement especially in investment and training. This debate will continue in the 1990s.

Notes

1. Brown, C.V. *et al.*, *Taxation and Family Labour Supply in Great Britain* (Dept of Economics, University of Stirling, 1987).
2. Bishop, M. and Kay, J., *Does Privatization Work? Lessons from the UK* (Centre for Business Strategy, London Business School, 1988).

8

International trade

The essence of international trade

So far we have focused largely on issues and policies relating to the domestic economy. This has involved the measurement of economic activity (national income accounting), the determination of national income (via the multiplier and accelerator effects) and the impact of various policy measures (fiscal, monetary and supply-side policies) upon the performance of the national economy. We now consider the impact of external factors upon the economy, thereby widening the analysis and understanding of the economy to include the reasons for and benefits from international trading relationships. The study of international trade has a long tradition within economics. The subject has attracted the attentions of the leading economists of the past three centuries and, to a large extent, their work on international economic problems has produced some of the most important tools of analysis used by modern economists. For example, early versions of the quantity theory of money (Chapter 6) were developed in the eighteenth century to explain the effects of gold flows linked to foreign trade on the level of domestic prices.

International economics has demanded greater attention from economists and businesses alike as the extent of world economic integration and interdependence has increased. Over the past three decades, the economies of North America, the European countries, Japan and the developing nations have become more and more dependent upon each other as sources of supply, e.g. raw materials, and as markets for goods and services. Inevitably this has meant that national governments are less able to formulate national economic objectives in isolation from the influence of activity in the rest of the world. The links between policies are even more significant in terms of the world's financial and capital markets, as witnessed every day when the reverberations on any one stock market are felt across the globe – recall how the crash of the New York Stock Exchange on 19 October 1987 ('Black Monday') swept across the world.

At the same time, the growth of international trade has allowed each participating national economy to use its resources more efficiently by concentrating production on those activities to which it is best suited and from which it gets the benefits of economies of scale. In this way, trade has raised real income in each country in the same way that specialization by an individual or firm generates greater returns. Trade is beneficial in other ways: for example, improvements in technology originating in one country are shared automatically with other countries through trade in goods embodying the technological advances. Such *technology transfer*, which is also associated with the growth of the multinational corporation, is an increasingly important vehicle for economic development today in many of the less-industrialized nations.

All firms are affected either directly or indirectly by international trade. The effects of this trade are felt in many forms: competition between firms for global or national market shares, availability of imported raw materials, the price of goods, investment opportunities worldwide, capital availability, employment prospects and so on. At the same time, these effects themselves are directly influenced by other forces, not least the effect of exchange rates on trade and competitiveness. This chapter provides an overview of international trade in the context of business. In particular, we examine the gains to be obtained from international trade for individual countries and the implications for economic development and firms. In reality, of course, not all countries aspire to *free* trading relationships, in the sense of trading without state interference. The growth of protectionist policies is also strong today. Conducting international business activities necessitates a clear understanding of the different motives for various policies. Hence, we examine the arguments for and against free trade and protection in order to provide a balanced view. The net result of international trade, at the macroeconomic level, is summarized in countries' balance of payments accounts. These provide an annual summary of the flows of goods and services as well as capital between countries. The make-up of the UK balance of payments accounts is explained in detail.

Since the mid-1980s, the UK has suffered from substantial deficits in its balance of payments accounts (see Chapter 2). Such deficits ultimately have implications for business activity and economic growth. Various policies are open to the government to try and arrest this problem; the main ones are identified here. Attention often focuses on the role of exchange rates to cure balance of payments deficits, but given the importance of exchange rates in international business a full analysis of their impact is reserved until Chapter 9. We begin this chapter by explaining in formal terms why most economists believe that substantial economic gains arise from international trade.

The principle of comparative advantage – an argument for free trade

Historically, countries began to trade with each other in order to make available to consumers in one country goods which were only produced in other countries. This is an oversimplification of trade today, however, since in practice the vast majority of goods and services traded are produced in many countries across the globe. This suggests that a more fundamental explanation for international trade exists. The fact is that not all countries produce goods with the same efficiency. This gives rise to the *principle of comparative advantage*, which demonstrates that trade is potentially beneficial to the economic welfare of a country if it specializes in the production of those goods and services in which it has a comparative advantage (i.e. the greatest relative efficiency). This principle can be readily illustrated by means of a simplified numerical example, highlighting, at least in theory, the gains for all countries participating in international trade.

Suppose two countries, A and B, both produce and consume two goods, say wheat and cars. Suppose that when both countries use all of their resources efficiently to produce only wheat, country A is able to produce 1,000 tonnes and B 2,000 tonnes. If all resources are switched to car production, both A and B are able to produce 500 cars each. This information is shown in Table 8.1. If we make the simplifying assumptions that factors of production are able to move freely between the production of wheat and cars within each country and that production of both can be varied without affecting average unit costs (i.e. constant cost production exists), then the production possibility frontiers facing A and B are as shown in Figure 8.1.

Unlike the production possibility curve shown in Figure 1.2, it will be

Table 8.1 Pre-trade output levels

	Wheat (tonnes)		Cars
Country A	1,000	or	500
Country B	2,000	or	500
Total world output	3,000	or	1,000

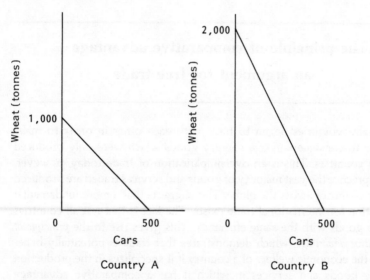

Figure 8.1 Pre-trade production possibility frontiers.

observed that the curves here are represented as straight lines. This arises from the assumption of constant cost production, introduced merely to simplify the discussion. To examine whether or not there will be any gains for both countries from trading with each other, we must consider each country's *opportunity cost* of production (i.e. what it forgoes by producing one of the goods).

In the case of A, resources can be used to produce either 1,000 tonnes of wheat or 500 cars. Thus, the opportunity cost of producing one extra tonne of wheat is 0.5 of a car. Similarly for B, 2,000 tonnes of wheat or 500 cars can be produced so that the opportunity cost of producing one extra tonne of wheat is 0.25 of a car. It is clear that country B is able to produce wheat at a lower *real* cost (in terms of cars) than country A. Therefore country B is said to have a *comparative advantage* in wheat

Table 8.2 Pre-trade output levels without specialization of production

	Wheat (tonnes)		Cars
Country A	500	and	250
Country B	1,000	and	250
Total world output	1,500	and	500

production. Conversely, if A produces one more car, the opportunity cost is 2 tonnes of wheat, while in the case of B it is 4 tonnes. Thus, A is said to have a comparative advantage in car production.

So far we have assumed that the resources in each country are devoted to either wheat or car production. Now let us assume instead that resources are divided equally to produce both wheat and cars, giving the outputs in each country as shown in Table 8.2 – with, as yet, no trade taking place between the countries.

Suppose now that an agreement to establish trading links is reached. Under what *terms of trade* will it be beneficial for both countries to agree to this trading link? Since for country A the opportunity cost of producing 1 car is 2 tonnes of wheat, then it will be happy to produce cars and exchange these for wheat provided the terms of trade exceed 2 tonnes of wheat for 1 car, i.e. provided A gets at least two tonnes of wheat for each car it sells. For B, the opportunity cost of producing 1 tonne of wheat is 0.25 of a car. Hence, B will be happy to produce wheat and exchange it for cars as long as the terms of trade are less than 4 tonnes of wheat per car, i.e. so long as the purchase of cars costs B less than 4 tonnes of wheat per car. If both countries agree to an exchange of, say, 3 tonnes of wheat per car, then both will gain by specializing and exchanging the good in which each has a comparative advantage. The outputs under specialization, before trade takes place, will now be as shown in Table 8.3.

It should be noted that the total output of wheat from A and B combined ('world output') has increased by 500 tonnes with car production unchanged, hence there has been a net gain. If A now exports 250 cars to B at an exchange rate of 1 car = 3 tonnes of wheat, then the two countries will be able to enjoy the consumption of the amounts of both goods as shown in Table 8.4.

Compared with the pre-specialization and pre-trade position shown in Table 8.2, both countries have gained in terms of additional consumption – A and B each have 250 tonnes more wheat and the same number of

Table 8.3 Pre-trade output levels with specialization of production[a]

	Wheat (tonnes)	Cars
Country A	0	500
Country B	2,000	0
Total world output	2,000	500

[a]With country A specializing in car production
and country B in wheat production, based on
the principle of comparative advantage.

Table 8.4 Pattern of consumption after trade[a]

	Wheat (tonnes)		Cars
Country A	750	and	250
Country B	1,250	and	250
Total world consumption	2,000	and	500

[a]Terms of trade: 1 car = 3 tonnes of wheat.

cars. The gains from trading can also be demonstrated by redrawing the
production possibility frontiers shown in Figure 8.1 (see Figure 8.2). It will
be seen that in both countries the frontiers have pivoted outwards,
representing a gain in welfare. These frontiers, as before, are drawn on the
basis of the amount of wheat *or* number of cars produced and consumed
if specialization of production and trade takes place. For example, the 500
cars produced by A are equivalent to 1,500 tonnes of wheat (with terms
of trade 1 car = 3 tonnes), while the 2,000 tonnes of wheat produced
by B are equivalent to about 667 cars.

Obviously, this example, which has been used to illustrate the principle of
comparative advantage and the gains from trade, has been greatly
simplified. Despite this, however, it provides a useful insight into why
countries should specialize in production. This applies even when they are
less efficient (in absolute terms) than another country in producing every
type of good. Countries should specialize in those goods in which they
have a *comparative advantage*. In addition, the principle lends support to
the case for free trade, i.e. trade without restrictions on imports or exports.

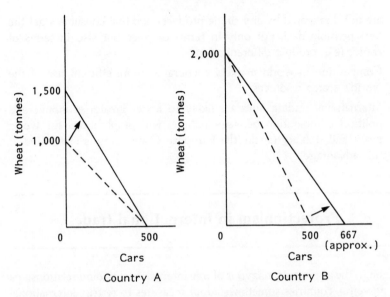

Figure 8.2 Gains from trade – post-trade production possibility frontiers.

Free trade combined with specialization results in an increase in the world's output, arising from the more efficient use of the world's resources; while this in turn has important consequences for economic development and hence for business expansion.

Further arguments for free trade

The principle of comparative advantage outlined above is the central argument used in support of free trading relationships between countries. As noted in the introduction to this chapter, however, there are other supportive arguments:

1. International trade, by creating larger markets for goods and services, benefits business through economies of scale in production (this particular argument is central to the principle of free trade within the development of the Single European Market).
2. International trade, devoid of restrictions, is likely to increase competition between producers, thereby helping to ensure that markets

are not dominated by any single producer and that consumers get the best possible deal, not only in terms of price but also in terms of choice (e.g. product differentiation).

3. Competition in world markets encourages more efficient use of the world's scarce resources.

4. International trading links are likely to foster greater economic and political co-operation between nations with implications for world peace and stability (again, the European Community is illustrative of this advantage).

Protectionism in international trade

Although the arguments in favour of free international trading relationships are powerful, countries sometimes adopt measures to restrict international trade. In this section we describe the most common forms of trade barrier and assess the arguments put forward in favour of protecting domestic industries from imports or providing some sort of state assistance, either directly or indirectly, to exporters.

Forms of trade restrictions

Trade restrictions can be applied by governments in a variety of ways, some of which may be openly identified while others may be 'hidden'. Restrictions may be categorized as follows:

1. Embargoes on imports.
2. Quotas on imports.
3. Tariffs or customs duties.
4. Other import restrictions.
5. Subsidies for domestic producers and exporters.
6. Exchange controls.
7. Exchange rate policy.

Embargoes on imports

These are the most extreme form of restriction on international trade, representing a total ban on the importation of certain types of goods or all goods from a particular country (such as the prohibition on goods from

South Africa imposed by many Commonwealth countries). The motives are often political, frequently as a defensive or retaliatory action against another country (for example, as in the case of the UK and Argentina following the Falklands War in 1982). From an economic viewpoint, embargoes deprive consumers of choice and industry ends by paying more for its raw materials, investment goods and components. The principle of trade according to comparative advantage is undermined and the overall result is likely to be a lower rate of economic development.

Quotas on imports

These are volume restrictions on imports whereby specific limits are set on the quantity of particular products that can be imported from one or more countries. However, while the immediate effect is to limit the volume of imported goods, domestic consumers face a limited supply which, if demand is strong, tends to force up the price of affected imports (and domestic alternatives), resulting in higher profits for the producer or seller. This has indeed been the experience with Japanese cars affected by 'voluntary' quotas (see below) sold in Britain with distributors often in the position of being able to sell at full retail price with little or no discount to customers. Similarly, US restrictions on microchip imports from Japan in the late 1980s served mainly to support the profit margins of the Japanese producers being squeezed by overproduction. American computer manufacturers lost out through higher prices for a basic component.

Tariffs or customs duties

These are taxes on imported goods which have the effect of raising the selling price to the domestic consumer with the tariff revenue going to the government (instead of to the seller as occurs with quotas when prices are raised). Tariffs may be *specific* (i.e. lump sum) in nature, or *ad valorem* (i.e. proportional to the value of the good). As with quotas, they can be applied to individual goods from individual countries or they can be applied more generally. The aim of tariffs is generally to discourage domestic residents from consuming particular imported goods by raising their price (though from the government's standpoint, the additional tax revenue may be an added incentive).

Other import restrictions

Apart from tariffs and quotas, governments may restrict the flow of certain imports by imposing a whole range of complex import regulations and documentation. Excessively high safety standards may be demanded of imported goods or just sheer bureaucracy may be used to slow down the volume of goods coming into the country. A classic example of such a restriction on trade involved the importation of Japanese video cassette recorders into France in the 1980s, when consignments were required to be transported to a remote location for 'quality' inspection (reputedly checked by an inadequate number of inspectors) thereby slowing down the release of the recorders onto the French market.

In the more difficult trading conditions since the 1970s many countries have also turned to 'voluntary' import restrictions. Tariffs and quotas often conflict with international trading agreements, notably the *General Agreement on Tariffs and Trade* (GATT) which exists to extend free trade. The UK was an initial signatory to the agreement in 1947. Voluntary controls on trade, however, subvert the spirit of the agreement without contravening its terms. The main victim of these controls has been Japan which has felt obliged, in the face of its growing balance of trade surplus with other leading industrial countries, to accept voluntary curbs on its exports. In particular, and as mentioned above, since the 1970s a voluntary quota has applied to the importation of Japanese cars into Britain. This has effectively limited the share of all Japanese manufacturers to below 11 per cent of the UK new car market.

Subsidies

By subsidizing the production of goods for domestic consumption as well as goods for export, governments attempt to maintain or increase the competitive position of domestic firms in the marketplace. Subsidies may be clearly identified (for example, regional development grants and investment incentives) or they may be hidden (such as relaxed planning restrictions). Exporters may be supported by government-backed guarantees against bad debts for overseas sales and may even receive direct financial assistance. All such forms of subsidy ultimately help to lower the price of goods produced by domestic firms and hence reduce competition from imports and assist exporters. This only applies, however, provided other countries do not adopt similar practices. Often, in fact, they do; which means that overall international trade may be little affected, while tax payers subsidize firms which benefit from higher profit margins.

Exchange controls

Governments may exercise control over the importation of certain commodities by imposing exchange control regulations. For example, exchange controls may limit the use of a country's foreign currency reserves to the importation of 'essential' goods and services only, thereby in effect blocking the importation of 'luxury' or non-essential goods (this policy is commonly adopted by developing countries to economize on the use of foreign reserves). Exchange controls may also be implemented in order to stem the flow of investment capital from a country, as in the case of the UK from the Second World War to their abolition in 1979.

Exchange rate policy

Perhaps less obvious than the methods above, a government may attempt to influence trade flows by devaluing its currency, thereby making imports more expensive in domestic markets while making its exports more attractive to foreigners. Such a policy is described as a *competitive devaluation*. Clearly, the extent to which the policy will be successful in stemming the flow of imports and boosting exports depends, among other things, on the sensitivity (*elasticity*) of demand for exports and imports to changes in their price and the extent to which the devaluation is unilateral. If two countries devalue their currencies by the same amount against each other, relative prices will remain unchanged. At the same time, the rise in the domestic price of imports will have an adverse effect on domestic production costs (imported raw materials and components cost more) leading to a rise in the general rate of inflation. This is an issue which we explore further in the next chapter.

Arguments in favour of protectionism

The arguments in favour of protectionism generally fall under one of the following headings:

1. Protection of infant industries.
2. Protection against 'unfair' competition.
3. Support for declining industries.
4. Support for strategic industries.
5. Retaliation.
6. Correction of balance of payments problems.

It should be appreciated, however, that the forces pressing for protectionism – producers and trade unions – are more likely to be motivated by self-interest than the public interest. At the same time, consumers who lose out from protectionism, through restricted choice and higher prices, are usually less well organized and vocal. Protectionism can therefore increase because of the power of vested interests – vested interests who attempt to justify their action in terms of the arguments below.

Protection of infant industries

It is sometimes argued that industries in the early stages of development need protection from competition in order that they can grow to a stage at which they can compete on equal terms with other countries' industries. This type of argument is generally accepted by economists as a valid reason for some of the restrictive measures described above, especially for new industries in developing economies. There is, however, a real danger that protecting infant industries makes them overreliant on state support, leading to sluggishness and inefficiency. Hence, the protection becomes permanent and the infant industry never matures. Equally, industries may be established behind tariff walls in countries where they have no long-term comparative advantage. Consequently, economic development becomes distorted and scarce resources are wasted.

Protection against 'unfair' competition

Producers often complain about unfair competition from firms in low-cost labour countries or because of subsidies granted to foreign producers by their governments. One particular form of unfair competition which attracted much attention in the 1970s and 1980s involves *dumping*, defined as the selling of goods abroad at 'uneconomically low' prices or below their production costs. The Americans and the Japanese clashed on this issue with regard to the importation of Japanese microchips into the USA in the mid-1980s, resulting in a spate of retaliatory measures (such as the temporary doubling of import duty on Japanese electrical goods into the USA).

At the same time, of course, dumping results in domestic consumers paying lower prices for the goods that are being imported, though this benefit should be weighed against the loss of jobs in domestic industries unable to compete with these lower prices. Therefore, the issue of dumping, like the issue of importing from cheap labour sources, largely becomes a question of balancing the effects on domestic employment and domestic prices. In practice, this involves not simply a cool economic evaluation of costs and benefits, but politicians deciding whether or not protectionist measures are politically acceptable to the electorate. It should also be appreciated that, from an economic perspective, cheap labour countries *should* specialize in producing goods which need abundant low-cost labour, for that is where their comparative advantage lies. This may be bad news for the textile industry in western Europe and the USA, for example, but the resources tied up in this industry (currently protected by a quota system under the Multinational Fibre Agreement within GATT) would probably earn a higher return utilized in the production of other goods and services.

Support for declining industries

Just as a rationale for protectionist measures is support for newly established industries, so protection is also proposed to ease the burden associated with declining industries (such as steel, coal, shipbuilding, etc. in the UK during the past twenty years). Most economists would argue, however, that protection in these circumstances should be short-lived since otherwise it arrests the decline of industries in accordance with changes in comparative cost advantages in production. Also, protection reduces the incentive to restructure and become more efficient to survive. Arguably, protection should be directed at easing the burden of adjustment associated with unemployment (especially regionally concentrated unemployment) while assisting the switching of resources into new industries and skills over a longer period of time.

Support for strategic industries

Certain industries, such as defence and aerospace, may be classified as being of strategic importance from a military perspective. Also, certain high-tech industries are sometimes classified as strategic because they are perceived to be of long-term importance in a country's economic development. Consequently, protectionist measures may be adopted to safeguard the future of such industries even if there are no immediate short-term benefits to be derived. This argument, however, contains many dangers, not least who decides what is a strategically important industry? In the early 1970s, UK toy producers called for protection from imports citing strategic arguments. They argued that the industry's production processes could be readily switched to munitions in wartime. Perhaps not surprisingly, the government at the time was unimpressed. Moreover, if a high-tech industry really is vital to a country's economic development, it would surely be expected to flourish in a free market.

Retaliation

An obvious argument in support of protectionism is that of retaliation against protectionist measures imposed by another country. The danger here, however, is a rapid escalation of protectionism on such a scale that world trade is curtailed – with severe consequences for world economic development. It would be much better if the countries concerned could find a way of dismantling the existing protectionist barriers rather than adopting self-defeating retaliatory measures.

Correction of balance of payments problems

Protectionist policies are often seen as a quick and easy means for a country to reduce its balance of trade deficit. Embargoes or quotas will be immediate in their effect, while tariffs or currency devaluation are likely to take time to reduce domestic demand for imported goods – the ultimate success of these measures being dependent on the responsiveness of demand to relative price changes (see Chapter 9).

The balance of payments

As has already been argued, international trade based on the principle of comparative advantage can be beneficial to all countries that take part in it. However, even armed with protectionist measures, international trade can present countries with balance of payments difficulties arising from a persistent mismatch in the flow of exports and imports. Countries with persistently large balance of payments deficits are likely to see their economic growth slow down as part of their national income flows to other countries, unless internally generated growth can compensate for this. At the same time, those countries with persistently large balance of payments surpluses, representing net injections into the circular flow of national income, may overheat as their economies reach capacity limits, unless new capacity can be developed or part of the surplus is invested overseas (a strategy that is now being followed by the Japanese through their huge investments in Europe, North America and many parts of the Far East). Furthermore, deficit countries are likely to experience a decline in the external value of their currency, while surplus countries are likely to experience a rise, both effects having important consequences for the flow of goods and services internationally. Clearly, the dynamics of international trade flows is a complex subject and we can but touch on the key issues here. We look first at the meaning of balance of payments.

The balance of payments is a summarized statement of a country's international trade transactions in goods and services and capital trans-actions with all other countries combined over a period of time. In the mid-1980s, some changes in the style of presentation were made to the

UK's balance of payments accounts. The latest version is presented here though we comment in passing on the changes that were made.

The UK's balance of payments account is broadly divided into two parts covering:

1. Current account transactions.
2. Changes in external assets and liabilities (formerly referred to as capital account transactions and including changes in official foreign currency reserves and borrowings).

By definition, the sum of these two parts of the balance of payments must be equal to zero (the overall balance of payments always balances). For example, a surplus of imports over exports might be financed by a reduction in official reserves or by international borrowing; in other words, by a fall in external assets or a rise in external liabilities. Similarly, a surplus of exports over imports might lead to a rise in foreign currency reserves or a repayment of past borrowings, leading to a rise in external assets or a fall in external liabilities. Media reports of a balance of payments deficit or surplus, therefore, should be clarified: they refer only to the situation on the *current account*. It is this part which reflects the difference between the value of goods and services imported and exported by the country during a given time period.

Current account transactions

The current account is subdivided for reporting purposes into transactions involving goods (denoted as *visibles*) and transactions involving services (*invisibles*). The visible balance is thus the difference between the value of exported *goods* from the country and the value of *goods* imported into the country, and is referred to as the *balance of trade*. The invisible balance consists of the sale and purchase of services between the UK and other countries, plus interest, profits and dividends received or paid, and other transfers. In more detail:

1. *Services.* These include transport services (such as shipping and aviation), banking services and other financial services (such as insurance) as well as estimated net receipts from tourism.
2. *Interest, profits and dividends.* These represent income receipts which arise from assets owned by UK firms in foreign countries (as well as payments to foreigners arising from their ownership of assets in the UK). These assets may be in the form of direct investments in

companies overseas, stocks and shares held in securities overseas as well as interest earned on lending abroad by banks.

3. *Transfers.* These represent the transfer of funds to other countries (or the receipt of funds from other countries), for non-trading and non-commercial transactions. They include private gifts and grants, subscriptions to or receipts from international organizations (such as the EC) as well as government payments to developing countries and for overseas military commitments, and certain other public and private sector international currency transfers.

External assets and liabilities

The other part of the UK's balance of payments account, comprising changes in external assets and liabilities over a given time period, is subdivided as follows:

1. *Changes in external assets.* These cover resident holdings of foreign currency or shares and other investments in overseas companies by UK residents, plus loans by UK banks to overseas borrowers.

2. *Changes in external liabilities.* These cover all investments in the UK by overseas residents as well as borrowing from abroad by anyone in the UK.

It should be noted that while the assets and liabilities are recorded in the *external* (formerly capital) account of the balance of payments for the period during which they have arisen, any eventual income or payment stream in the form of interest, profits and dividends appears under 'invisibles' on the current account. It is important to appreciate this point as it highlights the 'cost', for example, in terms of potential outflows on the current account from the UK in future years arising from large Japanese capital investments in the UK today, as well as the potential inflows from the UK's extensive investments overseas. Following the abolition of foreign exchange controls, UK overseas investments have increased from an estimated £12bn at the end of 1979 to £94bn at the end of 1988, making the UK reputedly the world's second largest overseas investor after Japan.

Table 8.5 shows the UK balance of payments account, based on the structure described above, for the years 1986–8. It should be noted that in the external assets and liabilities section, one item not mentioned so far is included in the subcategory for transactions in assets. This item is *official reserves.*

Transactions in official reserves

Transactions in official reserves consist of drawings on or additions to the country's official reserves (mainly gold and convertible foreign currencies), held by the Bank of England (and recorded in the *Exchange Equalization Account*). Traditionally, changes in these reserves were given prominence in the balance of payments statistics but nowadays less emphasis is placed on any changes. This has occurred because other international capital transactions have grown so dramatically in the last twenty years or so and are now, by value, extremely large in comparison.

Balancing item

The bottom line of Table 8.5 reports a balancing item. This relates to discrepancies between the total value of recorded transactions and the actual flow of money, i.e. it is the total of errors and omissions arising within the balance of payments accounts. Its value is known because the Bank of England's records show the net result of all foreign currency transactions. A positive value indicates that there have been unrecorded net inflows and a negative figure that there have been unrecorded net outflows. The size of the balancing item for any one year (as shown in Table 8.5) can be huge, highlighting the difficulties in interpreting the data for any single period. Indeed, it is probably fair to say that no other national income data are subject to errors as large as those involving the balance of payments.

Management of current account imbalances

We now turn to the consequences for a country that is experiencing a persistent balance of payments deficit or surplus and consider briefly what actions can be taken to correct the imbalance. This discussion provides a natural introduction to the analysis of exchange rates in the next chapter.

An imbalance with regard to the balance of payments will have the following implications. In the case of a deficit, the country will face a drain on its foreign currency reserves and is likely to find itself getting more and more into debt with overseas monetary authorities (recall the experience of the UK in 1976 when, following several years of huge

Table 8.5 The UK balance of payments accounts[a]

	1986 £m	1986 £m	1987 £m	1987 £m	1988 £m	1988 £m
Current account						
Exports	72,656		79,421		80,602	
Imports	82,020		90,350		101,428	
Visible balance		−9,364		−10,929		−20,826
Invisibles:						
Services	6,247		5,682		4,165	
Interest, profits, dividends	5,364		4,987		5,619	
Transfers	−2,181		−3,411		−3,575	
Invisible balance		9,430		7,258		6,209
Current account balance		66		−3,671		−14,617
UK external assets and liabilities						
Transactions on assets						
UK investment overseas	−34,373		−15,913		−24,937	
Lending by UK banks to overseas residents	−53,840		−50,322		−19,261	
Lending and deposits overseas by other UK residents	−2,782		−5,311		−3,035	
Official reserves	−2,891		−12,012		−2,761	
Other external assets of central government	−509		−796		−891	
Other external assets of UK non-bank private sector and public corporations	1,933		433		812	
		−92,462		−83,921		−50,073

Transactions on liabilities

Investment in UK by overseas residents	12,981	18,548	11,985
Borrowing from abroad:			
By UK banks	63,966	52,830	33,856
By other UK residents, including government and public corporations	3,804	2,007	3,567
Other external liabilities of central government	78	1,466	912
Other external liabilities of UK non-bank private sector and public corporations	539	1,402	2,089
	81,368	76,253	52,409
Net UK external assets and liabilities	−11,094	−7,668	2,336
Balancing item	11,028	11,339	12,281

a Adjusted to allow for rounding errors.
Source: CSO *United Kingdom Balance of Payments* (London: HMSO, 1989).

deficits, the then Chancellor Denis Healey went 'cap in hand' to the IMF to borrow funds to cover the UK debt position). This type of situation cannot, of course, persist indefinitely since both reserves and sources of borrowing are, ultimately, limited. In contrast, a country experiencing a continuous balance of payments surplus will be accumulating reserves at the expense of deficit countries. Consequently, it may be experiencing inflationary pressures in its domestic economy as the net inflow of currency boosts the domestic money supply (foreign currency inflows will ultimately be converted into sterling).

As we mentioned earlier, a deficit on the balance of payments will also tend to exert downward pressure on the country's exchange rate while a surplus will exert upward pressure. Whether or not the authorities permit the exchange rate to change at all and, if so, by how much, depends on the particular exchange rate policy that is being pursued (see Chapter 9).

Given these consequences of balance of payments imbalances, there are four possible courses of action that governments can take to correct them. (Any or all of these courses could be implemented to varying degrees at the same time.) They are:

1. Protectionist measures.
2. Demand management policies.
3. Supply-side policies.
4. Exchange rate management policies.

Protectionist measures, along with the arguments in favour and against, were discussed earlier in this chapter. Demand management policies could involve contractionary fiscal or monetary policies to reduce overall aggregate demand, including the demand for imports in the case of a balance of payments deficit. These contractionary measures could also reduce domestic inflationary pressures, thereby increasing the competitiveness of exports in world markets. On the other hand, a current account surplus could be reversed by pursuing expansionary fiscal and monetary policy measures, drawing in imports at a faster rate than the growth in exports. Broadly, if a country's rate of economic growth is faster than the average growth rate in its export markets then this will tend to cause imports to rise faster than exports through the *absorption effect* (the economy 'absorbs' more imports). In either of these situations, however, a conflict of macroeconomic objectives may well arise. For example, while deflationary measures may lead to an improvement in the current account deficit position, this may be achieved at the expense of high unemployment and low economic growth as aggregate demand slows down. Similarly, expansionary measures to reduce a current account surplus may stimulate inflationary pressures. Ultimately, the difficult choice of which objective takes priority – the balance of payments or the domestic economic environment – is decided by government.

As we saw in Chapter 7, supply-side policies are aimed at increasing the nation's output through greater productivity and other efficiency measures. It might be the case that a current account deficit has arisen because of a lack of competitiveness on the part of domestic firms in the world marketplace, resulting in a falling demand for exports and a rising demand for imports which substitute for inferior or more expensive domestic goods. This is a view commonly put forward to explain the repeated current account deficits experienced by the UK throughout most of the 1970s and again from the mid-1980s. Supply-side reforms may reverse this trend, though the process is likely to take many years. In the meantime, competitors are unlikely to be standing still.

Lastly, a current account deficit might be tackled by devaluing the currency against the currencies of international competitors. If the currency is 'managed' by the authorities (see Chapter 9), then they may engineer a devaluation. Alternatively, if the currency is allowed to float freely in the foreign exchange markets, so that its value depends entirely on the forces of demand and supply, it will decline automatically provided the supply of the currency being traded in the markets exceeds the demand for it. In the same way, the currency could be formally revalued or appreciate in the market when a country has a balance of payments surplus. It should be noted, however, that movements in the value of a currency are affected by factors other than trade flows, most notably by changes in external assets and liabilities brought about by short-term speculative movements of capital in and out of the country and longer-term flows in international investment. Therefore, there is no guarantee that a freely floating currency will lead to a balance on current account, as we see in the next chapter.

Concluding remarks

All businesses are affected by international trade whether directly, by being involved in importing and exporting, or indirectly because of the impact that the balance of payments has upon domestic economic activity.

One question which might run through a reader's mind at the end of this chapter is whether a current account imbalance matters.

There is no simple answer to this question, much depends upon what is happening to capital flows. Sustained imbalances in trade flows, unless offset by flows of capital, must eventually trigger changes in national income. If the UK has a current account deficit which is financed by an inflow of investment funds from abroad then the imbalance is sustainable, especially if the capital inflow is long-term investment (short-term investment is much more of a problem because it can quickly flow out again — what is called a flight of *hot money*, precipitating a currency crisis). The USA in the latter part of the nineteenth century ran current account deficits financed by inflows of capital (from Britain and elsewhere) which went, for example, into building America's railroads. Similarly, Japan has maintained its large export surplus in the 1980s, without causing an even larger rise in the value of the yen against other currencies than has taken place, by investing large amounts of its surplus international earnings abroad.

One issue which we have explored at some length in this chapter has been the protection of domestic producers from imports. Not surprisingly, those working and investing in industries directly threatened by imports tend to favour protectionism. On the other hand, and as we have seen, protectionism imposes major costs on consumers when they are denied access to cheaper and superior imports. Also, it can lead to inefficiency as competitive pressures are reduced. Most economists agree that competition is the key to high efficiency.

9

Exchange rate policy

The essence of exchange rate policy

The previous chapter considered the importance of international trade in business and economic development and showed how trade and capital flows give rise to a country's balance of payments account. At the end of the chapter a number of problems associated with deficits or surpluses in the balance of payments were identified along with possible solutions. We now turn to study the last of these solutions: changing the exchange rate.

The need for exchange rates arises because one country's currency is usually not acceptable as a medium of exchange in another. For example, a British exporter will want to be paid for his goods in sterling because his workers and suppliers are unlikely to accept foreign currency. The foreign buyer will therefore have to obtain sterling in order to pay for the British goods, offering his own currency in exchange. Alternatively, the British exporter may accept the foreign currency but will then convert it into sterling. The same process occurs, in reverse, when British firms import goods from overseas. Also, today, much trade in the world takes place in a third currency, notably the US dollar which in effect acts as a go-between for the exporter's and importer's currencies.

International trading relationships therefore result in a demand for and supply of currencies. This in turn has led to the development of sophisticated foreign exchange markets, for example in New York, Tokyo and London, to co-ordinate the millions of interactions of demand and supply decisions that take place every day, leading to the determination of exchange rates between currencies. Not all currencies, however, are freely exchangeable (convertible) with other currencies. Non-convertible currencies (for example the Russian rouble) are sometimes referred to as soft currencies as opposed to the hard currencies of the major western countries.

There are many types of exchange rate policy which countries can adopt: the choice will be determined by the nature of the economic stance taken by governments and the problems faced. In essence, the policies may be categorized under three headings:

1.   A floating exchange rate system.
2.   A fixed exchange rate system.
3.   A managed exchange rate system.

In this chapter we describe the mechanics of each system and discuss the case for each in terms of its viability and effectiveness. The choice of exchange rate system is a major issue in economics today given the degree of international integration which has evolved in recent years. Exchange rates have obvious and important implications for businesses, especially those involved in exporting and importing. It is important, therefore, that managers appreciate not only how exchange rates are determined but their impact on the macroeconomic environment in which businesses operate. Hence, in this chapter we also discuss the role of exchange rate policy in the correction of balance of payments imbalances and conclude by considering how managers can attempt to minimize the effects of changes in exchange rates on their business.

Exchange rate systems

Floating exchange rates

Under a floating system, a country's exchange rate is determined solely by the demand for and supply of its currency in the international foreign exchange markets. In other words, it is determined just like the price of any good or service in a free market. A floating exchange rate system, by definition, therefore, results in an *equilibrium* rate of exchange which will vary continuously as demand and supply forces change. When a currency's exchange value rises as a result of market forces, the exchange rate is said to *appreciate*; when its value falls it is said to *depreciate*.

The process by which currencies float up or down is illustrated in Figure

Figure 9.1 Floating exchange rates.

9.1. In Figure 9.1(a) the initial equilibrium exchange rate for sterling in terms of the US dollar is shown as $1.65 and arises from foreign exchange transactions totalling £Q_1. Suppose now that the demand for sterling rises as a result of an increased demand for British exports. This is shown as a shift in the demand schedule for sterling from D_1D_1 to D_2D_2. Consequently, sterling appreciates from $1.65 to $1.80 as the amount of sterling exchanged increases to £Q_2, everything else being equal. It will be appreciated that had the demand for sterling fallen, say, due to a decline in British exports, this would have caused the demand schedule for sterling to shift to the left leading to a decline in the $/£ exchange rate.

In Figure 9.1(b), again the initial exchange rate is $1.65 but this time there is an increase in the supply of sterling, from S_1S_1 to S_2S_2, on the foreign exchange markets. This could arise, for example, if there was an increase in British demand for foreign goods. Everything else being equal, the $/£ exchange rate will depreciate to $1.50. Once again, it should be recognized that a reduction in the supply of sterling on the foreign exchanges would have led to an appreciation in sterling's value.

The above analysis of the determination of exchange rates is based upon the assumption that there is no government intervention in the foreign exchange markets. The methods by which governments can intervene are discussed below with reference to *fixed* and *managed* exchange rate systems. In other words, we have been concerned with *pure* or *free* floating exchange rates. Also, we have linked movements in exchange rates solely to changes in the demand for and supply of exports and imports. In practice, however, exchange rates are determined by a whole range of factors, as discussed on pages 183–7.

Fixed exchange rates

At the other extreme to a free floating exchange rate system, lie fixed exchange rates. A government may pursue a policy of keeping the external value of its currency fixed at a stable rate by intervening in the foreign exchange markets. This intervention is carried out using official reserves to balance the demand for and the supply of the currency in order to maintain the particular exchange rate at a given level. For example, as illustrated in Figure 9.2(a) an increase in the demand for sterling from D_1D_1 to D_2D_2 could be offset by the authorities augmenting the supply of sterling from S_1S_1 to S_2S_2 (to buy dollars for example) in the foreign exchange markets, in order to counteract the upward pressure on the value of sterling. Conversely, as shown in Figure 9.2(b), a decrease in the demand for sterling from D_1D_1 to D_2D_2 could be offset by the authorities by, for example, restricting the supply of sterling to the market from S_1S_1 to S_2S_2. The end result of both of these actions is that the value of sterling is held at the fixed exchange rate of $1.65.

The maintenance of fixed exchange rates in the manner just described requires that the authorities hold sufficient reserves or have access to sufficient loans for intervention purposes. In the UK the responsibility for intervening lies with the Bank of England which manages the country's foreign reserves under the guidance of the Treasury.

The gold standard

During this century there have been two periods in which fixed exchange rate systems have prevailed in the world economy. The first lasted in one form or another up until the early 1930s and was known as the *gold*

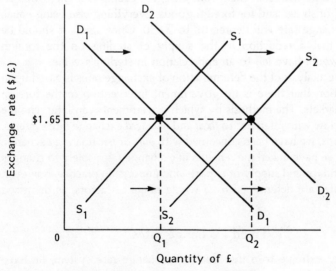

Figure 9.2 Fixed exchange rates.

standard. Under this system the value of each currency was fixed in terms of an amount of gold. This necessarily meant that the value of any particular currency was fixed in terms of any other currency. In addition, international trade was primarily financed by gold shipments and the internal money supply was broadly determined by the amount of gold held by central banks. Basically, therefore, when exports exceeded imports, more gold flowed into the country than out. Consequently, the internal money supply rose, which in turn led to upward pressure on prices (see Chapter 6 and the quantity theory of money for a discussion of the link between the money supply and prices), which in turn caused exports to become less competitive and imports more so. This process would continue until exports equalled imports and the gold inflow, therefore, ended. A similar mechanism operated in reverse when imports exceeded exports; gold would flow out of the country, the money supply would contract and prices would fall until, again, exports and imports were in balance.

It must be stressed that this is only a brief summary of the principles of the gold standard. In practice, occasional devaluations of currency values against gold occurred and central banks did intervene from time to time to ameliorate the economic effects of gold flows. Nevertheless, up until the outbreak of the First World War the gold standard permitted a high degree of automatic balance of payments correction. It broke down in the inter-war years, however, largely because, with the growth of trade unions and large firms, wages and prices proved less easy to adjust downwards than in the nineteenth century. Therefore, output rather than prices declined as gold flowed out leading to reduced employment. Governments facing rising unemployment in the early 1930s finally abandoned the gold standard.

In general, economists today rule out a return to the gold standard largely for reasons of practicality. On political grounds it would not be internationally acceptable to rely on gold which is mined principally in the Soviet Union and South Africa, but there are also economic reasons. Under completely fixed exchange rates, surpluses and deficits in the balance of payments can be corrected only by changes in relative prices in the countries concerned or, if prices are inflexible, by reducing or increasing national income. For example, a country with a balance of payments deficit would need to deflate demand to the extent needed to reduce imports sufficiently to bring them into balance with export revenues. A country running a balance of payments surplus can continue to add to its foreign reserves, but a country with a deficit will sooner or later run out of reserves. For every deficit in the balance of payments of one country there must be an equal and offsetting surplus in the balance of payments of other countries. In principle, therefore, both deficit and surplus countries should act to correct payments imbalances. In practice, the burden of adjustment falls on the country running a balance of payments deficit to deflate its national income.

The Bretton Woods system

The second period of fixed exchange rates this century lasted from the end of the Second World War to the early 1970s. It emerged from a meeting of the allied powers at a conference at Bretton Woods, New Hampshire in 1944, and hence is often referred to as the Bretton Woods System. Following the collapse of the gold standard in the 1930s, countries had attempted to gain competitive advantage by reducing their exchange rates, making exports relatively cheap and imports more expensive. Such action was primarily intended to boost employment prospects and was commonly referred to as a 'beggar my neighbour policy'. Ultimately, these measures damaged world trade.

At Bretton Woods it was agreed that fixed exchange rates should be restored but that a return to the gold standard was undesirable. A proposal advanced by the US delegation (the *White Plan*) formed the basis of the scheme finally endorsed. Under this scheme, all currencies were assigned a fixed exchange rate against the US dollar (a dollar parity), which in turn was assigned a fixed value against gold ($35 per troy ounce for official transaction purposes). As a consequence, cross exchange rates between currencies were fixed. The link between the US dollar and an officially recorded volume of gold acted as a break on the printing of surplus dollars by the US government and therefore maintained confidence in the US dollar.

The Bretton Woods system was not entirely a fixed exchange rate regime since currencies were permitted a small degree of flexibility (± 1 per cent against the dollar parity until 1971). Large adjustments, however, could take place only where there were fundamental disequilibria in balance of payments (i.e. persistent and large deficits or surpluses) and only by agreement with member countries (though this latter condition was not always met). The system was supervised by an international body also established at Bretton Woods, namely the *International Monetary Fund* (IMF) based in Washington. Where countries suffered temporary balance of payments deficits, governments were expected to intervene in the foreign exchange markets to preserve the fixed parity using their foreign reserves. These reserves could be augmented by borrowing from the IMF up to agreed limits or from other central banks. At the same time, countries were expected to correct their balance of payments disequilibria by appropriate domestic fiscal and monetary policies – deficit countries deflating and surplus countries reflating. In practice, once again, the burden fell mainly on the deficit countries since the surplus countries lacked the same pressure to act.

In the case of the UK the sterling exchange rate was devalued only twice from 1945 to 1972. Once in 1949, when sterling was devalued from $4.03 to $2.80, and again in 1967 when the parity was reduced to $2.40. This contrasts vividly with experience under floating exchange rates which the UK adopted in June 1972. Since then the sterling exchange rate has fluctuated widely against the dollar and other currencies. The same is true for other leading currencies, which also abandoned fixed exchange rates in the early 1970s. Note that not all of sterling's fluctuation against the US dollar has been due to factors affecting the UK. Since the dollar floats up and down too, movements in the $/£ rate often occur because the dollar is changing in value on the international markets. This point should always be borne in mind when interpreting movements of sterling against any particular currency. It also explains why, in the media, sterling is sometimes quoted in terms of a basket of leading currencies or, more correctly, the *sterling exchange rate index* which is a trade-weighted average of seventeen currencies. Movements in this rate are more likely to reflect fundamental changes in the external value of sterling (changes in the exchange rate index since 1979 were illustrated in Figure 2.9 in Chapter 2).

The Bretton Woods system broke down for a number of reasons. Briefly, there was a growing lack of international liquidity; the main currencies held in central bank foreign reserves were the US dollar and, to a declining extent, especially after the 1967 devaluation, sterling. World reserves could finance 48 weeks' exports in 1948 but only 14 weeks' worth by the mid-1970s. This was exacerbated by declining confidence in the US dollar. To expand international liquidity, central banks had to be willing to hold dollars in their foreign reserves. There were no difficulties while confidence in the dollar was maintained. However, rising US government expenditures overseas (e.g. the Vietnam War) as well as the financing of America's space programme and the establishment of its social welfare system (the 'Great Society' programme) in the 1960s, led to a flood of dollars onto world markets and confidence sagged. In particular, dollars were traded for gold which was considered to be a secure asset. At this time, however, gold had a fixed price under the Bretton Woods system of $35 per troy ounce, which the US government was committed to protect.

In 1968, following widespread conversion of dollar holdings into gold at the fixed rate by many countries, the US had to concede defeat and a two-price system for gold was introduced under which central banks continued to transfer gold among themselves at $35 per troy ounce, while gold was allowed to find its own value in the free market for non-official purposes. With a worsening US balance of payments on current account, however, this provided only a short respite. In August 1971, official dollar convertibility had to be suspended temporarily following renewed speculative activity. In December 1971 the Smithsonian Agreement officially devalued the dollar against other currencies and against gold (from $35 to $38 per troy ounce). Since other currencies were expressed in terms of the dollar, this meant that new currency parities were established (for sterling $2.67 = £1). This agreement was itself quickly overwhelmed, however, by world economic events. Rising inflation aggravated by a 500 per cent increase in world oil prices between 1971 and 1975, which undermined the balance of payments accounts of the leading industrial economies, meant that the Bretton Woods system finally collapsed. Governments turned to floating their currencies, usually in the form of a *managed float*.

Managed exchange rates

A managed exchange rate system refers to a situation where exchange rates are determined in the main by the conditions of demand and supply, but central banks intervene from time to time to stabilize the rates or influence them in some way. Thus if sterling is depreciating rapidly the authorities would sell foreign currency reserves and buy sterling, helping to reduce the downward pressure. Similarly, to reduce an appreciating sterling value, the authorities would sell sterling and buy foreign currencies. In this way, intervention will help to smooth out the fluctuations in the exchange rate.

It should be appreciated that the degree to which the authorities are able to neutralize all fluctuations and hence keep the currency at a fixed rate, is limited. Central banks do not have sufficient reserves or lines of credit to intervene over a long period in foreign exchange markets, especially since around $600bn worth of currencies are traded each day. Consequently, a degree of flexibility in the exchange rate may have to be accepted. Managed flexibility can take a number of different forms such as *dirty floating* and *joint floating*.

In dirty floating, the decision as to when to intervene to support the currency and to what extent, is arbitrary. Some commentators argue that this describes the position taken by the UK authorities in the late 1980s when sterling came up against considerable downward pressure. The main objective, however, under dirty floating is to have reasonable stability in the exchange rate in order to maintain confidence in the currency – and perhaps in the government's general macroeconomic policy. The term dirty floating arises because governments attempt to 'manage' the float through foreign exchange intervention. An alternative, and less pejorative term, is a *managed float*.

Following the collapse of the Bretton Woods system of fixed exchange rates, a number of European countries set up a *joint float* in 1972 which became known as the *snake*. Under the snake, currencies were pegged to each other but were allowed a maximum variation between any two of the participating currencies of $\pm 2\frac{1}{4}$ per cent. They were then allowed to float freely (or within a band) against other currencies. At first the snake was a joint float against the dollar though this link was broken in 1973 and it essentially evolved into a small 'club' of European currencies shadowing the Deutschmark.

In 1979, the snake arrangement was replaced by the *European Monetary System* (EMS). This system is still very much in operation today and has a major role to play in the development of the Single European Market. Further details of the EMS are given in case study 3 in Chapter 10 but, briefly, the system is an extension of the snake in that member currencies are managed so that they remain within margins of $\pm 2\frac{1}{4}$ per cent (the Spanish peseta has a wider margin of ± 6 per cent) against each other as well as against the *European Currency Unit* (ECU). The ECU is a *basket* unit of account whose value is derived as a weighted average of EMS member currencies, including sterling, the Greek drachma and the Portuguese escudo, though the UK, Greece and Portugal have yet to become members of the EMS *Exchange Rate Mechanism* (ERM) for stabilizing currency movements. The EMS has built into it a number of features which have helped to ensure the relatively smooth adjustment of exchange rates towards values which more accurately reflect the underlying economic conditions of the member countries. It should be noted that the UK did not participate fully in the EMS arrangements from its inception because of fears that membership might prove unsustainable. The value of sterling was especially volatile in the late 1970s and early 1980s when the UK achieved petro-currency status following North Sea oil discoveries. Again, we return to the central issues in this debate in Chapter 10.

Exchange rate systems compared

In this section we set out the central arguments both in favour and against the adoption of fixed or floating exchange rates. Clearly, there is no simple answer as to which system is best: the choice will depend upon current economic conditions and, perhaps, the political philosophy ruling at a given point in time (free market versus intervention).

The case for floating exchange rates

The main attraction of adopting a floating exchange rate system is the apparent *automatic adjustment* to balance of payments problems. For example, if a country is experiencing inflationary problems which foster an adverse balance of payments, then depreciation of its currency should compensate for a loss of price competitiveness in international markets and pull the balance of payments back towards equilibrium. Similarly, if a country is running a surplus on its balance of payments, an appreciation in the exchange rate will raise the price of its exports and reduce the price of its imports until the balance of payments is back in equilibrium.

Since floating exchange rates should automatically rectify a balance of payments problem, there will be less need for a country to pursue demand management policies to reduce the demand for imports (i.e. to reduce imports through the absorption effect referred to in Chapter 8). The country will then be free to devote greater attention to solving internal problems (e.g. unemployment). At the same time, there will be less need for large reserves to be held by the authorities since the exchange rate does not have to be supported. All of these conclusions, however, only apply provided an appreciation or depreciation of the currency is not managed by the authorities but reflects demand and supply pressures in the foreign exchange markets. Also, a floating system does not guarantee a balance of trade flows because daily demand for and supply of leading currencies are more influenced by capital flows (including speculative activity relating to currency movements) than trade flows.

The case against floating exchange rates

Leaving aside the possibility that floating exchange rates may reflect movements of capital rather than trade flows (indeed capital movements may have a perverse effect on the balance of trade – see case study 5 in Chapter 10 which considers the US balance of payments), their main drawback lies in the uncertainty created in international trading and investment. This is particularly important for businesses. For example, if a British exporter invoices a foreign buyer in his own foreign currency, he will not be sure how much he will receive when this foreign currency is converted into domestic currency. However, such exchange rate uncertainty can be mitigated – at a price – by the use of *forward exchange contracts*, discussed later in this chapter (pages 186–190).

Floating exchange rates could also discourage some investors from investing overseas. This is more likely to be the case when exchange rates move erratically in large jumps leading to possible major capital losses – as well as potential capital gains, of course – when the investor realizes his investment or when interest, profits and dividends are remitted. The international investor faces exchange rate risk in addition to the usual risks attached to any investment activity. Again, the use of forward exchange contracts would mitigate this uncertainty.

The case for fixed exchange rates

Perhaps the strongest argument in favour of fixed exchange rates is that they impose some discipline on domestic monetary systems. For example, if a country's exports become uncompetitive and there is a balance of payments deficit, the authorities will have to resort to deflationary policies to improve the country's international payments position. Supply-side measures are also likely to be implemented, encouraging the restructuring of domestic industries. It has been suggested that the decline in sterling's value during the past twenty years provided little incentive for British industry to face up to the harsh reality of the need to restructure and invest in new plant and equipment. In other words, the depreciation of sterling simply extended product life cycles and outmoded working practices but could not put off the inevitable. Moreover, in so far as a depreciating currency permits an exporter to pass on production costs, notably large wage settlements, a floating exchange rate system is not conducive to defeating domestic inflation. The UK Treasury's desire to hold sterling firm after 1986 owed much to the view that British industry should not be 'bailed out' by a sterling depreciation if it gave way to excessive wage demands (i.e. wage demands not paid for out of productivity gains).

The case against fixed exchange rates

As discussed earlier, fixed exchange rates may be maintained by the authorities by intervening in the foreign exchange markets, but this requires large amounts of foreign currency reserves. In practice, central banks have finite loan facilities and reserves (the Bank of England, for example, held foreign reserves to the value of $34.8bn in December 1989, down from $44.1bn a year earlier following extensive intervention in the markets to support the value of sterling). At the same time, as the world's capital markets have expanded and opened up in recent years, the extent to which any one government is able to intervene to counteract the huge volumes of capital that now flow around the world is extremely limited. Even the seven leading countries known as the *Group of 7* or G7 (UK, Japan, USA, Canada, Italy, France and West Germany) acting in concert have not always been able to forestall currency movements. Ultimately, as the saying goes, 'you cannot buck the market'. Therefore, irrevocably fixed exchange rates may be unrealistic today. The gold standard and the Bretton Woods system operated at a time when much smaller volumes of currency were traded daily and a much larger proportion of foreign exchange transactions were trade related. The Bretton Woods system collapsed because of widespread speculation against leading currencies, notably the US dollar.

There are two further arguments against fixed exchange rates. First, since the exchange rate is fixed any changes in international competitiveness cannot be reflected in currency movements. Therefore, the burden of adjustment to improve competitiveness must fall on the domestic economy through industrial restructuring, wage restraint and deflationary policies. Second, in attempting to keep the exchange rate fixed in the face of market forces the authorities lose control over the domestic money supply. This occurs because the money supply has to accommodate the fixed exchange rate. For example, in order to halt an appreciation in the value of the currency, the authorities might intervene by selling sterling in the foreign exchange markets. This sterling, however, will then tend to find its way back into the domestic economy thereby boosting the money supply. This in turn will add to inflationary pressures. Alternatively, interest rates might be reduced to stem capital inflows to the country but this will tend to encourage domestic credit expansion as people borrow more at the lower interest rates. Hence, the adoption of a fixed exchange rate system results in a loss of control over monetary policy – this is a major reason for the UK government's reluctance to take up full membership of the EMS by participating in the ERM.

The loss of UK monetary control in this context was graphically demonstrated in 1987 and 1988 when the then Chancellor of the Exchequer Nigel Lawson attempted to 'shadow the Deutschmark' (at around DM 3 = £1). At the time market pressures were pushing up sterling's value above this rate. Consequently, the authorities expanded the sterling money supply through foreign exchange intervention and by reducing UK interest rates and this contributed to a loss of control over the domestic money supply with, as witnessed in late 1988 and after, serious consequences for UK inflation.

Why does currency speculation occur?

We have referred to currency speculation in the foreign exchange markets on a number of occasions so far in this chapter. A simple example will help to underline why it can be very profitable and therefore why it occurs. Suppose that a speculator (an individual, a bank or a company with surplus funds) sold sterling to the sum of £100m on the foreign exchange market and bought US dollars, when the exchange rate was $2 = £1. The speculator would receive $200m. If this transaction reflected a general market tendency to sell sterling and buy dollars, the pound would *depreciate* against the dollar (or looking at it another way, the dollar would appreciate against the pound). Suppose the rate of exchange settled at $1.80 = £1, the speculator could now repurchase £111m with the $200m holding ($200m/ $1.80). The profit on the transaction (ignoring costs such as trading commission and tax) is £11m.

Of course, if the speculator had judged the mood of the market incorrectly and sterling had *appreciated* against the dollar, instead of depreciating, then a loss would have resulted. Currency speculation carries inevitable risk unless the direction of change in the exchange rate can be predicted with complete certainty. Under the Bretton Woods system of fixed rates, the likelihood of a currency revaluation was low while a currency under selling pressure might well be devalued. Speculation, therefore, was often 'a one-way bet'. Under floating rates, however, currencies can just as easily go up in value as down. From this brief discussion, it should be obvious why governments deny that they would like to see the value of their currency fall in international markets, while not intervening extensively to prevent a fall (such as the UK in 1989). Any suggestion that a government harboured a desire to see its currency decline in value would trigger-off a bout of speculative selling because the future movement of the currency is more predictable.

The determination of exchange rates

So far we have been analyzing different types of exchange rate system and the arguments for and against the adoption of each. A government, as a formal policy or on an *ad hoc* basis, may influence the value of its country's exchange rate relative to other currencies; also, the exchange rate is affected by the flow of exports and imports of goods, services and capital into and out of a country. However, there are a large number of other factors which interact within the economy to affect the external value of currencies and we now examine these.

At the macroeconomy level, changes in national income have an impact upon the demand for imports as well as goods and services produced for the domestic market which might otherwise be exported if demand for them did not exist in the home market. Changes in aggregate demand are therefore reflected in the demand for and supply of currencies on the foreign exchange markets and, hence, in exchange rates. At the same time, supply-side factors play an important role. The ability of an economy to increase output and employment eventually has implications for its balance of payments and ultimately its exchange rate.

Apart from the general state of the macroeconomy, both on the demand side and on the supply side, there are two further economic variables which have a direct impact upon exchange rates. These are:

1. The rate of domestic inflation relative to that in other countries.
2. Domestic interest rates compared with competing interest rates abroad.

The rate of inflation and the exchange rate

In general, differences in the rates of inflation between countries will be reflected in the exchange rates between their currencies. Countries experiencing higher rates of inflation will tend to experience depreciation in the external value of their currencies. The converse applies to countries experiencing lower rates of inflation than average; their exchange rates will tend to appreciate. These movements tend to occur gradually under freely floating exchange rates, but more slowly and falteringly where rates are managed or fixed because the authorities intervene to offset market movements, in ways already discussed.

Observations on the apparent inverse relationship between inflation rates and exchange rates led to the development of *purchasing power parity theory*. This attempts to explain changes in currency values exclusively in terms of relative rates of inflation in different countries. In essence, the theory predicts that the exchange rate of one currency against another currency will depend upon the *relative purchasing power* of these currencies in their own countries. For example, if £1 buys X amount of goods in the UK and $1.60 also buys the same X amount of goods in the USA, then the equilibrium exchange rate should be £1 = $1.60. If this is not the case, and ignoring transport and freight insurance costs, then goods will be imported from the cheaper country, creating a balance of trade deficit in the more expensive country, whose currency will tend to fall in value until the equilibrium rate is established. Thus, purchasing power parity theory states that an exchange rate varies according to relative price changes, so that:

$$Old \text{ exchange rate} \times \frac{\text{Price level in country A}}{\text{Price level in country B}} = New \text{ exchange rate}$$

The theory, however, has proved inadequate as an explanation of movements in exchange rates in the short term. In part this is because it ignores the importance of transport, insurance and other costs in assessing relative costs of goods. But also, relative costs and prices of non-traded goods included in the measurement of domestic inflation rates make comparison of these inflation rates unreliable in determining exchange rate equilibria. Nevertheless, purchasing power parity theory has been shown to have more validity in predicting the *long-term* movements of exchange rates. Countries that persistently experience relatively high inflation rates eventually also experience depreciation in the value of their currencies on the foreign exchange market under a floating exchange rate regime.

Interest rates and exchange rates

A strong link is also evident between interest rates and exchange rates. For example, high interest rates in one country relative to other countries will tend to attract inflows of capital from these lower interest rate economies (unless there are other factors acting as a disincentive to invest, e.g. political instability or a perception that the exchange rate of the country is about to fall). These capital flows will, in turn, raise the exchange rate of the recipient country. This relationship is particularly significant in the world's money and foreign currency markets today in equalizing interest rate differentials between the major international financial centres, as discussed in the following example which introduces the role of the forward exchange market.

Suppose that capital is allowed to flow unhindered between the USA and UK and that a three-month deposit of capital can earn a 14 per cent return in New York and a 10 per cent return in London. The 4 per cent margin between the returns will, everything else being equal, entice UK investors (speculators) to move sterling from London to New York, investing perhaps in short-term US dollar deposit accounts. This action requires them to *sell* sterling and *buy* dollars at the current (spot) exchange rate between the dollar and sterling. As a consequence, the supply of sterling will rise as the demand for the dollar rises, leading to an appreciation in the dollar's value and a fall in sterling's value on the foreign exchange market.

It is possible that during the three-month deposit period, the value of the dollar could fall sharply (for whatever reason) against sterling. The consequent capital loss could then outweigh the greater return earned through the 4 per cent interest rate differential. To protect against this possibility, the UK investor could cover his liability by dealing in the *forward exchange market*. That is, he could buy dollars against the spot exchange rate for sterling, and simultaneously agree to sell dollars against sterling *three months forward*. This is known as a *forward contract*. The difference between the quoted spot and forward exchange rate is known as the *forward premium* (or *discount*) which will be incorporated in the forward rates quoted by the UK exchange dealer, i.e. the dollar premium will be deducted (and dollar discount added) to the $/£ spot exchange rate. It should be noted that the size of this premium or discount must exactly equal the difference between dollar and sterling interest rates (in this case 4 per cent) otherwise an opportunity will exist for *arbitrageurs* to make money by buying or selling in the spot or forward markets. It follows that forward exchange rates are determined by interest rate differentials rather than simply by market expectations of exchange rates in the future.

The example above also highlights the extent to which speculation in foreign exchange can itself be a stabilizing influence on exchange rate values. For example, if a country has a balance of payments deficit on its current account then there will be downward pressure on its currency. If speculators take the view that such a deficit is only temporary, then they may be tempted to buy the currency when it is falling in value and sell again when its value rises as the balance of payments returns to surplus later – hoping, of course, to make a profit in the process as detailed earlier in this chapter. In this way, any depreciation in the currency will be offset to some extent by the buying decisions of speculators.

In contrast, speculation may also be destabilizing, particularly where the volumes of currencies being bought and sold are so huge that they lead to changes in currency values that are not reflective of the underlying economic reality, i.e. exchange rates may *overshoot* or *undershoot* equilibrium levels. On balance, many economists would argue that excessive speculation is destabilizing by creating uncertainty about currency values which, as we noted earlier, may damage international trading relationships and hence world trade and growth. On the other hand, this type of speculation is difficult to distinguish from sound commercial decisions by financiers, including corporate treasurers. If they believe a currency will shortly decline in value then it makes sense to sell the currency now. Recall, however, that the action of selling a currency, perhaps based upon a rumour in the markets that the currency is coming under pressure, has the effect of *causing* the value of the currency to fall.

Exchange rates and the balance of payments

On several occasions we have noted, generally, that floating exchange rates can correct a balance of payments imbalance: the adjustment should be automatic via the market mechanism. Demand for a surplus country's currency will be rising, pushing up its exchange rate and thus making its exports more expensive and its imports cheaper. In this way the balance of payments surplus will tend to be eliminated while the reverse process can be expected in the case of a deficit country.

In practice, this seemingly automatic mechanism does not always appear to work – or, if it does, it takes time for the effects to become evident. This situation is typical of that which has often faced the UK: despite a fall in the sterling exchange rate against nearly all other major currencies, the balance of payments continues to be a problem. Why?

When currencies depreciate, it may take time for people to adjust their patterns of consumption and to change their investment plans. For example, British households and firms may continue to buy what they regard as high quality imports, despite the fact that a fall in sterling's value may have pushed up import prices. At the same time, foreigners may not respond immediately to the fall in sterling by placing immediate orders for UK goods – again, tastes and preferences take time to change. Thus, the responsiveness (i.e. elasticity) of demand for both imports and exports as a consequence of changes in currency value may be quite sluggish. This implies, therefore, that depreciation will lead to an improvement in the balance of payments if the sum of the price elasticities of demand for exports and for imports exceeds unity. This condition is popularly known as the *Marshall–Lerner condition*.[1]

If the Marshall–Lerner condition is not satisfied then, in fact, as the currency of a deficit country falls in value, the initial effect may be a *worsening* in the balance of payments. In other words, given that the

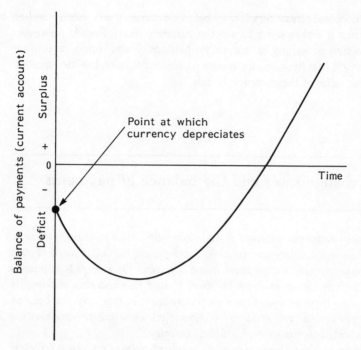

Figure 9.3 J-curve effect.

volumes of imports and exports are likely to remain unchanged in the short term, the total import bill (valued in domestic terms) will be rising faster than the total revenue from exports (valued in domestic terms) as the currency depreciates. Indeed, if exports are originally priced in sterling, then with demand unchanged the sterling revenue will stay the same. Hence the balance of payments can deteriorate initially, as illustrated in Figure 9.3.

However, as Figure 9.3 also suggests, in time the balance of payments position is likely to improve as demand for the now cheaper-priced exports expands (assuming that the foreign price of the exported goods is reduced to reflect the depreciation) and as demand for the now more expensive imports falls. In other words, depreciation eventually leads to an improvement in the balance of payments, giving rise to the *J-curve effect* as shown in the figure. Economists have estimated that it may take on average eighteen months for the UK balance of payments to start to improve following a depreciation in sterling.

Of course, the opposite logic applies in the case of surplus countries facing an appreciation in their currencies. In the short term, if demand is

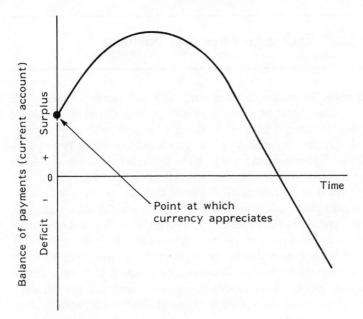

Figure 9.4 Inverted J-curve effect.

sluggish to respond to relative price changes, appreciation is likely to boost the balance of payments surplus further. Eventually, however, it is to be expected that the volume of imports and exports will respond to the price changes as shown in Figure 9.4. This is known as the *inverted J-curve effect.*

As noted earlier, despite a general fall in sterling's external value against a number of leading currencies, the UK's trade performance has deteriorated in recent years. This suggests that factors other than relative prices are important in determining the extent to which a balance of payments deficit can be reversed. Indeed, some economists argue that price considerations are often given too prominent a place in explanations of trade flows. They stress a number of other reasons for the weakness in Britain's balance of payments position. It is argued, for example, that UK manufacturers have failed to move up-market over the last two decades in terms of quality, design and marketing, restricting the growth in exports and encouraging import penetration. In other words, it is stressed that *non-price* factors have been dominant, reflecting the slow pace of structural change and supply-side inflexibility in British industry. It remains to be seen whether the so-called Thatcher Revolution of the 1980s has brought about sufficient change in the supply-side of the economy to improve Britain's balance of payments position in the 1990s.

Exchange rates and business

Erratic changes in exchange rates can, as noted earlier, increase the uncertainty facing management in its decision making. Given the likelihood of a lengthy time period between winning an export order or placing an import order and the final delivery of the goods and the settling of accounts, exchange rate fluctuations can make all the difference between a profit or a loss on the transaction. In this way, floating exchange rates may discourage trade and investment decisions though, as discussed above, short-term risks can be overcome by the use of forward exchange markets, where firms can agree to buy currency at a given future date at a contracted price. This will, however, involve transaction costs such as commission. Forward contracts cannot usually be negotiated for more than a year in advance, so they cannot be used to cover longer-term risks in international trade and investment. Other methods to reduce exchange rate risk include:

1. Use of *forecasts* of exchange rate movements.
2. *Risk-spreading* through having a range of overseas suppliers and export markets trading in different currencies, in the hope that this will provide some security.
3. *Hedging,* which is useful where there is no forward market; a corporate treasurer can deal in foreign currencies and deposit sums in different currencies as a hedge against currency fluctuations.
4. *Investing in foreign subsidiaries:* multinational companies reduce exchange rate risk by sourcing and supplying in various countries; exchange rate movements may also lead them to reallocate work between national plants to retain competitiveness and to protect profits.

Fluctuations in exchange rates require managers to make difficult economic decisions. This is illustrated by the following example. Suppose a UK firm is exporting a luxury car selling at £20,000 in the UK and, at an exchange rate of $1.75 = £1, $35,000 in the USA (ignoring freight and insurance charges, etc.). If the company currently sells 1,000 vehicles per annum in the USA, its total earnings there are $35m. Now suppose that the exchange rate *appreciates* to $2 = £1, the UK manufacturer faces two choices:

1. To continue to sell in the USA at the existing price of $35,000 but now receiving only £17,500 as against £20,000 per vehicle in sterling

($35,000 ÷ $2). Hence total receipts fall by £2.5m (£17.5m as against £20m).

2. To raise the US price to compensate for the sterling appreciation. The price of vehicles in the USA would therefore rise to $40,000. But at the higher price fewer cars are likely to be sold.

Which of the two options will be chosen depends upon the *price sensitivity of demand* (or *elasticity*) for the vehicles in the USA. If they are price sensitive then raising the price to $40,000 might lead to *lower* sales receipts in sterling than if the price had been left unchanged. For example, if vehicle sales fell to 750 per annum, total revenue in sterling would be £15m (750 × $40,000 ÷ $2). A similar managerial decision would have to be faced if the currency *depreciated*: in this case whether to reduce the overseas sales price by an equivalent amount or whether to sell at the same price but with a healthier profit margin in sterling terms. Again, the price sensitivity of exports will be an important deciding factor. Also relevant are expectations as to how long the depreciation will last (there is no point in reducing prices today and then increasing them again next week), and whether the firm has sufficient capacity to produce more output for export (there is no point in stimulating export sales through price reductions which cannot be met).

Concluding remarks

Fluctuating exchange rates affect production costs if imported raw materials and components are required. At the same time, downward pressure on the currency may lead to higher domestic inflation which is likely to feed through into higher wage demands, with implications for employment, profits and investment plans.

Movements in exchange rates add a further and unwelcome element of risk and uncertainty in business decision-making today. For this reason many people in business demand greater exchange rate stability. But stable exchange rates (within or outside a mechanism such as the EMS) have pitfalls as well as advantages. Without exchange rate flexibility, cost and price increases in excess of those experienced in competitor countries must lead to a decline in exports and a rise in imports. The consequent deterioration in the balance of payments will lead government to introduce economic measures designed to deflate demand and thus reduce economic growth to bring down inflation. This is likely to feed through into lower profitability, plant closures and unemployment.

At the same time, however, floating exchange rates may not be the answer. Floating rates may be inflationary, in the sense that they enable governments to postpone remedial action to reduce inflationary pressures; while depreciation increases the prices of imported goods which adds to inflation. For this reason some economists would welcome the UK's early entry into the EMS Exchange Rate Mechanism. Once sterling's rate against the other member currencies is fixed then the UK authorities, to maintain the rate, must bring the country's inflation rate close to that of the other members, and notably the much lower rate existing in West Germany.

Note

1. In its simplest form this states that the price elasticities of demand for exports and imports must sum to more than unity if a fall in the external value of the currency is to lead to an improvement in the balance of payments. This follows because the volume of exports increases and the volume of imports decreases as export prices fall (denominated in foreign currency) and import prices increase (denominated in domestic currency) when the exchange rate falls. *Elasticity* is simply a numerical measure of the responsiveness of demand with respect to these price changes. If the price elasticity of demand for exports plus the price elasticity of demand for imports exceeds unity, then the increased cost of imports (in terms of the domestic currency) is outweighed by the value of the growth in exports. Hence the balance of payments improves.

10 Case studies

These case studies are intended to test the reader's understanding and awareness of the concepts and principles covered in this book. They cover a wide range of topics dealing with both domestic and international economic issues and end with a series of questions for individual consideration or class discussion. Intentionally, we have not included specimen answers: first, because the complexity of the economy is such that there is no such thing as an absolutely right way of managing the economy, and second, because we do not want to pre-empt class discussion where the book is being used on business and management courses.

The cases deal with the following aspects of the macroeconomy:

1. Interpreting national income data.
2. The relationship between inflation and unemployment.
3. Britain and the European Monetary System.
4. The international debt crisis.
5. Analysis of the US twin deficits.
6. Linkages between money, growth, prices and interest rates.
7. Outlook for the economy.

Other cases may be found in some of the books listed on page 220 as further reading.

1   Interpreting national income data

We saw in Chapter 3 that national income figures have a number of uses. One use is as a guide to differences in the standard of living between countries and the way that standards of living vary between countries over time.

Table 10.1 gives details of gross domestic product (GDP) per head in US dollars and in real (price-adjusted) terms for a number of major economies between 1960 and 1987. Supplementary information is also supplied from national income accounts on real private consumption per head.

Questions

1. What is meant by the term 'standard of living'?

2. On the basis of the figures in Table 10.1, what do you think has been happening to the standard of living in the UK relative to other countries since 1960?

3. What further information would you ideally require to make a more definitive judgement as to comparative standards of living?

2   The relationship between inflation and unemployment

In an article published in 1958, A.W. Phillips indicated on the basis of UK data for the period 1861–1957 that there was a strong negative relationship between the rate of change of money wages and the level of unemployment. The statistical analysis indicated that the relationship had been remarkedly stable for a continuous period of almost a hundred years with a higher unemployment rate being associated with a lower rate of growth of money wage rates. Soon after the original research was completed, it was also argued that there was also a significant and stable negative relationship between the rate of change of prices (i.e. inflation) and the level of unemployment. This is not really surprising since wage increases not paid for out of higher productivity are likely to be passed onto consumers in the form of price increases. Hence the correlation between wage and price inflation is likely to be statistically high. This relationship between the growth of wages and prices on the one hand and unemployment on the other has become known as the *Phillips curve* (see Figure 10.1).

Table 10.1 International comparison of living standards

	GDP per head[a]				Private consumption per head[a]			
	1960	1970	1980	1987	1960	1970	1980	1987
Canada	5,681	7,897	10,934	12,674	3,287	4,224	6,055	7,050
USA	7,798	10,006	11,804	13,535	4,739	6,203	7,557	8,914
Japan	2,670	6,487	9,069	11,226	1,752	3,724	5,336	6,287
Australia	6,096	8,372	10,137	11,282	3,714	4,862	5,998	6,450
France	6,114	9,457	12,335	13,409	3,610	5,481	7,262	8,217
W. Germany	7,215	10,276	13,216	14,703	3,668	5,504	7,413	8,320
Greece	1,460	2,882	4,164	4,327	1,051	1,909	2,688	2,926
Italy	3,831	6,244	8,081	9,173	2,214	3,860	4,954	5,789
Norway	6,723	9,364	14,121	17,098	3,722	4,951	6,700	7,977
Portugal	1,005	1,861	2,701	2,946	773	1,332	1,818	2,000
Spain	2,431	4,455	5,674	6,375	1,587	2,874	3,760	4,032
Sweden	8,689	12,718	14,938	16,727	5,066	6,810	7,733	8,610
Switzerland	10,560	14,329	15,920	17,276	6,294	8,504	10,125	10,763
UK	6,387	7,935	9,521	11,044	3,881	4,624	5,660	6,887
OECD total[b]	5,528	8,017	9,975	11,369	3,299	4,755	6,060	6,979
EEC total	5,286	7,775	9,847	10,939	3,045	4,524	5,878	6,632

[a] All figures in US dollars at 1980 values.
[b] Includes all of the above countries plus New Zealand, Austria, Belgium, Denmark, Finland, Iceland, Ireland, Luxembourg, Netherlands, Turkey and Yugoslavia.
Source: OECD, *National Accounts 1960–1987*, vol. 1 (Paris, 1989). pp. 130–1.

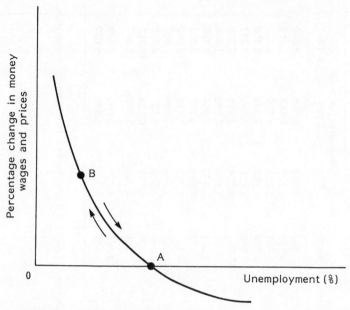

Figure 10.1 The Phillips curve.

The work of Phillips seemed to offer government a range of policy choices. It suggested that governments could trade-off a particular level of unemployment against a particular rate of inflation. For example, if aggregate demand were stimulated (say, via tax cuts and/or an expansion of government spending), this could reduce unemployment but at the expense of a higher rate of inflation and vice versa. In other words, governments could fine-tune aggregate demand and push the economy up and down the Phillips curve (say from A to B and then back to A again). Furthermore, it was suggested that unemployment could not be reduced below its natural rate shown as point A in Figure 10.1. As we saw in Chapter 2, this natural rate is associated with equilibrium in the labour market where the demand for labour at a given real wage rate is equal to the supply of labour – any unemployment remaining is 'natural' in the sense that those out of work either do not want to work at the going wage rate or their services are no longer in demand (because of structural changes in the economy; this is referred to as *structural* unemployment). Some workers will also be temporarily out of work due to the fact that the transition from one job to another may not be instantaneous (referred to as *frictional* unemployment), or due to seasonal factors.

For much of the 1960s many governments actively attempted to manage their economies on the basis of the Phillips curve relationship. It provided

Figure 10.2 UK wage growth and unemployment 1970–89.

an attractive policy choice which could be triggered at suitable times (perhaps reducing unemployment in the run-up to elections). However, towards the end of the 1960s the relationship began to look unstable as unemployment, wages and prices all began to rise together. Figure 10.2 plots the rate of wage growth against the unemployment rate for the UK for the period 1970 to 1989 along with the original Phillips curve. During the 1970s there was, in fact, a marked outward shift in the relationship with stagflation being a prominent feature of the economy (rising unemployment associated with growing inflation). Through the 1980s, under the Thatcher administration, inflationary pressures have resided and unemployment has dropped significantly but the UK economy is still, today, a long way from the original Phillips curve as shown in Figure 10.2.

There has been considerable debate concerning the reasons for this apparent breakdown of the original Phillips curve, stimulating much research on the economics of the labour market and the causes of inflationary pressures.

Questions

1. What explanations can you give for the apparent collapse of the Phillips curve:
   (a) During the 1970s?
   (b) During the 1980s?

2. What evidence is there to suggest that a trade-off between unemployment and inflation is likely to re-emerge in the 1990s in the UK?

3   Britain and the European Monetary System

At its meeting on 6 and 7 July 1978, the European Council under the presidency of Roy Jenkins (a member of the UK Labour Party at that time) agreed that closer monetary co-operation between European Community (EC) countries should be promoted through the creation of the European Monetary System (EMS). The EMS was designed to establish within the EC an area of currency stability based on closer monetary co-operation and a convergence of economic policies. It was formally established on 13 March 1979 and, since its birth, has surprised many of its former critics by coping with the pressures and turbulent changes in exchange rates during the 1980s.

At the heart of the system is the Exchange Rate Mechanism (ERM) which establishes the limits within which the value of member countries' currencies are allowed to fluctuate. At present, nine EC nations participate in this arrangement, but it is intended to bring the three non-participants (Britain, Greece and Portugal) into the scheme during stage 1 of the 1989 EC plan for economic and monetary union (commonly referred to as the Delors plan after Jacques Delors, former president of the European Commission). ERM members are obliged to keep their currencies within narrow limits. Limits are set for each currency around central rates established against the European Currency Unit (ECU), and against the other participating currencies in a cross rate grid.

The ECU is a composite currency containing fixed amounts (a 'weighted basket') of each of the twelve EC currencies, as shown in Table 10.2. These fixed amounts are reviewed by the EC every five years and can be changed only by official action. The weights of the twelve currencies are calculated by converting their fixed amounts into common currency at current market exchange rates. This means that a currency's weight can move in response either to a change in its fixed amount or to a change in its market exchange rate. Official recompositions are intended to correct changes in ECU weights caused by currency movements which cannot be justified by underlying economic criteria. The last recomposition took place on 21 September 1989 (as shown in Table 10.2) when the ECU basket was enlarged to include the Spanish peseta and Portuguese escudo. In between these official recompositions, a currency's ECU weighting, and so its *effective* weight in the ECU, will fluctuate in step with changes in market exchange rates (see below). These market-induced changes in ECU weights will remain small

Table 10.2 Composition of the European Currency Unit

	ECU percentage weightings at recomposition			Fixed currency amount in ECU 21 Sept. 1989	US$ exchange rate 9 Feb. 1990	US$ value value 9 Feb. 1990	Effective weighting 9 Feb. 1990
	13 Mar. 1979	17 Sept. 1984	21 Sept. 1989				
Deutschmark	33.0	32.0	30.1	0.6242	1.6725	0.373	30.6
French franc	19.8	19.0	19.0	1.332	5.6780	0.235	19.3
Pound sterling	13.3	15.0	13.0	0.08784	0.5935	0.148	12.1
Italian lira	9.5	10.2	10.15	151.8	1244.0	0.122	10.0
Dutch guilder	10.5	10.1	9.4	0.2198	1.8865	0.117	9.6
Belgian franc and Luxembourg franc	9.7	8.5	7.9	3.431	35.0	0.098	8.0
Danish krone	3.1	2.7	2.45	0.1976	6.4350	0.031	2.5
Irish punt	1.1	1.2	1.1	0.008552	0.6315	0.014	1.2
Greek drachma	—	1.3	0.8	1.440	157.35	0.009	0.7
Spanish peseta	—	—	5.3	6.885	108.60	0.063	5.2
Portuguese escudo	—	—	0.8	1.392	147.80	0.009	0.7
						ECU 1 = $1.219	

in the absence of a realignment of ERM central rates. Since the 21 September 1989 recomposition, the effective weight of the Deutschmark, for example, has increased from 30.1 to 30.6 per cent (as at 9 February 1990) – see Table 10.2.

From Table 10.2, it will be seen that an ECU is defined as the sum of 0.6242 Deutschmarks, 1.332 French francs, 0.08784 sterling, and so on. The table also shows the actual exchange rate between each of the twelve European currencies and the US dollar (as at 9 February 1990). Dividing each ECU weighting by the corresponding exchange rate translates the contribution of each member currency of the ECU into US dollar terms. Hence, it will be noted that by summing these dollar values, ECU 1 was equivalent to US$1.219 on 9 February 1990. Each contribution, as a percentage of the US$/ECU value, results in the effective weightings within the ECU of each member currency.

As noted above, each currency within the ERM has a fixed central rate which establishes bilateral parities or cross rates. Currencies are allowed to fluctuate by $\pm 2\frac{1}{4}$ per cent either side of these limits (with the exception of Spain which has been given a ± 6 per cent margin; Italy also had this wider margin but adopted the narrower range in January 1990).

A major innovation within the EMS is the *divergence indicator* which is a type of early warning system that is triggered when the value of one currency moves out of line with its agreed central rate against the ECU by more than 75 per cent of the permitted margin. The divergence indicator for the Deutschmark, for example, with a 30.1 per cent weight in the ECU, is set at $\pm 75\% \times 2.25\% \times (100 - 30.1) = \pm 1.1796\%$, whereas the divergence limit for the Irish punt (with a 1.1 per cent weight in the ECU) is set at $\pm 75\% \times 2.25\% \times (100 - 1.1) = \pm 1.6689$ (in effect a more generous margin than for the Deutschmark). Once the divergence indicator is reached, the central banks of the currencies concerned are expected to take remedial action, for example by supporting their currencies using official reserves or adopting deflationary or expansionary economic policies. In this way, the system is designed to ensure that surplus and deficit countries are treated symmetrically, i.e. the burden of adjustment is shared by the strong as well as the weaker members of the system. The essential purpose of the divergence indicator, therefore, is to identify those countries whose domestic policies are expansionary or contractionary relative to the average policies of all member countries. Countries with a growth in national income or interest rates, which influence capital flows into and out of member countries, out of line with other members' levels, will tend to find that their exchange rates begin to diverge from their agreed values. Hence, under the ERM, a convergence of economic performance within the EC is anticipated.

The EMS arrangements also provide for an extension of the credit facilities available to member countries to facilitate central bank support of exchange rates. But an ultimate aim within the EMS and endorsed by the Delors plan is the creation of a single European Central Bank to co-ordinate credit facilities and the conduct of economic policies of member countries. In the meantime, however, a European Monetary Co-operation Fund (EMCF) exists to manage these matters.

From the outset, Britain has refused to join the Exchange Rate Mechanism and thus bring sterling within the full membership of the EMS. Britain is, however, involved in the credit arrangements that are available and sterling is a constituent currency of the ECU as indicated in Table 10.2. The British government has persisted in its view that 'now is not the right time' for Britain to become a full member throughout the 1980s and has therefore adopted a jaundiced view of the 1989 Delors Report's recommendations that all the EC countries should quickly become full members of the ERM, and that sooner rather than later positive progress should be made towards full monetary union within the EC.

Questions

1. What benefits might Britain enjoy by joining the Exchange Rate Mechanism of the EMS?

2. What reasons can you give to explain the British government's resistance to membership?

3. What other benefits may arise from the continued development and strengthening of the EMS from the viewpoint of Europe in general?

4. Some members of the EMS are concerned that if Britain does not join the exchange rate arrangements soon, then the volatility of sterling on the foreign currency markets may be destabilizing for the EMS. Why?

4 The international debt crisis

Following a more than quadrupling of world oil prices between 1972 and 1974, the oil exporting countries of the Middle East were left with large current account surpluses in their balance of payments. To offset this, they were encouraged by western governments and banks to invest their surpluses in the world capital markets. The western banks acted as financial intermediaries, recycling these funds to borrowing countries. Chief among the borrowers were the 'middle income', less developed countries (LDCs), notably Argentina, Venezuela, Brazil and Mexico. These countries were benefiting at the time from buoyant world prices for their commodities, notably raw materials, and had an apparently insatiable demand for external funds for private investment and government spending. By 1982, when the debt crisis broke, the total indebtedness of non-oil-exporting LDCs stood at $814.4bn.

The onset of world recession in 1979, however, led to a fall in the prices of most raw materials. Oil exporting debtor nations, such as Venezuela and Mexico, benefited from a further rise in oil prices in 1979–80, but faced special problems from 1986 when the price of oil fell from over $27.80 a barrel in 1985 to around $13. Economic difficulties were compounded by higher interest rates on debt resulting from tight monetary policies pursued in the industrialized countries to bring down their inflation rates. Major debtor nations experienced an appreciation in real interest rates of 45 per cent between 1979 and 1982. In turn, higher interest rates in the USA led to an appreciation in the value of the US dollar in which most of the international debts were denominated, aggravating even further the problems facing debtor nations.

Faced with a deteriorating economic situation in the debtor countries, the inflow of new capital into these countries declined sharply from 1982 onwards. The resulting flight of capital added to the foreign exchange burden of funding interest payments. Since 1984, instead of capital flowing from the industrialized countries to the LDCs, there was actually a net outflow of funds from the LDCs to the industrial countries. In August 1982 the debt crisis broke when Mexico called a moratorium on its debt repayments, triggering similar action in a number of other debtor countries. Since debts have to be serviced out of foreign exchange, one useful measure of the debt burden is interest payments as a ratio of export earnings. Normally, a ratio of over 20 per cent is considered difficult to service without imposing serious strain upon an economy. In 1986 the fifteen most heavily indebted LDCs operated with ratios averaging over 43 per cent. Consequently, these countries have had to deflate domestic demand so as to switch from running trade deficits to registering trade surpluses and their economic growth rates have stagnated (see Table 10.3).

The economic implications of the international debt crisis since 1982 have extended beyond the debtor countries and their exporters to the western banking system. In 1984 the nine largest US banks had outstanding LDC debts equivalent to 263 per cent of their capital. Initially, the banks attempted simply to reschedule the debts, but more recently the banks have had to accept that many of the debts will never be repaid. By early 1989, West German banks had made bad debt provisions in the order of

Table 10.3 Economic performance of LDCs

	1973–9 (average) %	1983–8 (average) %
All LDCs		
Percentage export volume growth	2.6	4.7
Percentage import volume growth	8.5	−3.1
Fifteen most heavily indebted LDCs		
Percentage real growth in GDP	5.9	1.9

Source: International Monetary Fund.

Table 10.4 Third World debt provisions of major UK banks

	Percentage of total outstanding debts		
	31 Dec. 1988	30 June 1989	31 Jan. 1990
Barclays	38.0	48.0	70.0
Lloyds	34.0	47.0	72.0
Midland	32.6	50.4	50.2
National Westminster	35.0	48.4	65.0

Source: Financial Times, various dates.

50 per cent of their LDC debts; French banks 45 per cent; Canadian banks 35 per cent; and US banks 30 per cent. In the UK, the bank most exposed to LDC debts has been the Midland Bank, although all of the major banks (excluding the TSB) have significant exposure. Against these debts the banks have had to increase their bad debt provisions in the late 1980s as it became obvious that there was little likelihood of full repayment (see Table 10.4). This has not been achieved without pain. For example, because of these bad debt provisions the Midland Bank in 1988 became the first UK clearing bank since the war to record a loss in its annual accounts. Although the western banking system is today more capable of weathering a spate of major international debt defaults than it was in the early to mid-1980s before bad debt provisions were made, such an event would still cut a swathe through bank balance sheets. Reputedly, Manufacturers Hanover, for instance, the US bank with the largest exposure to LDC debts, would have had only around one-third of its equity left if it had marked down all of its Latin American loans to their current market value in 1989. Major Latin American default on international debt (perhaps now compounded by defaults by the new governments of heavily indebted eastern Europe) could still trigger a major crisis in western banking.

Questions

1. What effect is the international debt crisis likely to have on the world economy?

2. What solutions might be considered to manage the crisis?

3. What lessons are there for companies operating internationally as a result of the growth of international indebtedness?

5   Analysis of the US twin deficits

Since 1980 the USA, the world's largest economy, has become the world's largest debtor. Large budget deficits under President Reagan and now under the Bush administration have resulted in a trebling in the US national debt. The rise in the budget deficit is detailed in Figure 10.3. An underlying structural deficit (government spending exceeding taxation) was compounded in the early 1980s by a cyclical deficit reflecting a downturn in the US economy (more government spending and a lower than expected growth in tax revenues). Later, as the economy recovered, increases in government spending, notably defence and tax cuts in 1982 introduced to stimulate the supply-side of the economy, served to keep the overall budget deficit at historically high levels.

Worries in Congress eventually led in 1985 to the passing of the Gramm–

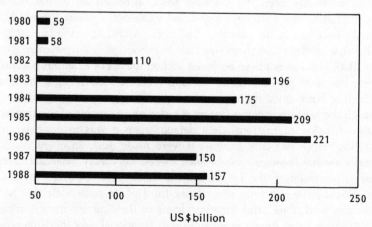

Source: US Congressional Budget Office

Figure 10.3 US budget deficits.

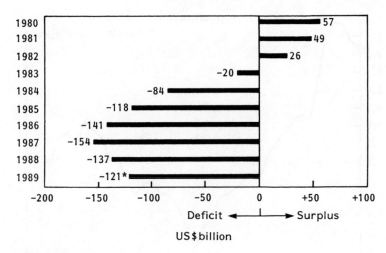

*Estimate.

Source: US government.

Figure 10.4 US balance of payments – current account.

Rudman–Hollings Act which established budget deficit targets for each fiscal year. The aim was to reduce the deficits until 1991 when the budget would be balanced. Either the administration would make the cuts voluntarily, and thereby preserve priority spending, or under the Act automatic cuts would apply across all departmental budgets. The Act had a discouraging start, however, when the Supreme Court ruled it unconstitutional. It was only in 1987 that an amended Act with revised targets took effect.

High interest rates have been one important result of the large budget deficits, as the US administration has resorted to tapping world savings. This has tended to push up interest rates in other countries competing for international capital. As international investors have scrambled to buy dollars to invest in US Treasury securities, this has driven up the value of the US dollar on the foreign exchanges. Consequently, US exports have been made less competitive and imports more competitive, resulting in a large and persistent US current account deficit (see Figure 10.4). As a percentage of GDP, the US current account went from a surplus of 0.2 per cent in 1981 to a peak deficit of 3.2 per cent in 1986, before falling back to between 2 and 3 per cent in the late 1980s. The appreciation of the US dollar was temporarily reversed after 1985 when the US central bank, the Federal Reserve, brought the value of the US dollar down by increasing the money supply and bringing down interest rates. A resultant

An appreciation of the dollar against sterling is shown by a falling
$/£ exchange rate, while a dollar depreciation is shown as a rise

Figure 10.5 Fluctuations in the $/£ exchange rate.

rise in inflation, however, meant that this policy was abandoned in 1988,
and the dollar appreciated again (as illustrated in Figure 10.5 against
sterling).

The twin deficit problem is treated seriously by US public opinion.
Roughly one-eighth of the vastly expanded US national debt, around
$350bn, is now owned by foreigners (this is over three times as large as
the foreign debt of Mexico or any of the other heavily indebted LDCs
referred to in the previous case study). The speedy and substantial switch
from the US having large net external assets to having record net external
liabilities in the 1980s (valuing all assets at historic cost) is resented in the
USA. Also, recent inflows of capital have not merely gone into financial
securities, but into US buildings, land and industry. In particular, Japanese
ownership of physical assets in the US has threatened to produce a
nationalistic backlash there.

The budget deficit is often perceived to be the cause of the large balance
of payments deficit on current account. Some economists have even
suggested that the US balance of payments deficit cannot be eliminated
until the government's budget is balanced. We can better appreciate this
argument if we use and develop some of the basic national income
accounting introduced in Chapter 3. The gross national product or output

(GNP), ignoring the import content, is made up of goods bought by consumers (C), government (G), firms for investment (I) and foreigners in the form of exports (X), i.e.:

$$GNP = C + I + G + X$$

Similarly, the national income is spent, giving rise to gross national expenditure (GNE), on domestically produced consumer goods and services (C) or saved (S) or it can be taken in tax (T) or spent on imports (M), i.e.:

$$GNE = C + S + T + M$$

(In both of the above equations C is expressed net of expenditure taxes and subsidies.) Since GNE must equal GNP by definition (see Chapter 3) and since C is common to both of the above equations, it follows that:

$$I + G + X = S + T + M$$

Rearranging into sectors of the economy – international trade (X and M), the capital market (S and I), and the government sector (G and T) – we can express this last equation in the form:

$$(X - M) = (S - I) + (T - G)$$

From this we can see that if the government increases its budget deficit $(T - G)$ and the difference between private saving and investment $(S - I)$ stays constant, then any gap between total domestic leakages from the circular flow of income $(S + T)$ and total domestic injections into the circular flow $(I + G)$ must rise (for an explanation of injections and leakages see Chapter 4) and so, therefore, must the current account deficit $(X - M)$; i.e. M will exceed X as imports are sucked into the economy). This result, whereby a balance of payments deficit arises from an increase in domestic aggregate demand (as the consequence of, say, a budget deficit), arises from the *absorption effect*, i.e. imports are 'absorbed' into the economy. Everything else being equal, to rectify the balance of payments deficit the gap between T and G can be reduced either by raising taxes or by cutting public spending (or both). Alternatively, by holding spending at around current levels, if national income is rising, *fiscal drag* (see Chapter 5) will lead to higher tax receipts and this in time will reduce the budget deficit significantly. (This approach to cutting the deficit avoids some hard political choices and not surprisingly is the preferred option of the Bush administration.)

The idea that cutting the budget deficit will improve the US balance of payments position depends crucially, however, upon the gap between I and S staying unchanged. In the 1980s, all major economies have experienced a decline in household savings – in the case of the USA from around 8 per cent of disposable income in 1980 to a low of 3 per cent in 1987. Should private sector savings, including non-personal (i.e. corporate) savings, fall and private investment rise or stay constant then the gap between I and S will increase, in turn worsening the balance of payments position. Indeed, it should be appreciated from the sectoral equation above that if investment expenditure exceeds savings then a current account balance (where expenditure on exports equals expenditure on imports) *requires* the government to run a budget *surplus* equal to the difference between I and S.

The US budget deficit has worsened the country's balance of payments position, but from the above discussion it should be obvious that balancing the budget does not guarantee that balance of payments problems will disappear. Also, we might ask what would be the ramifications for the UK and other leading trading nations if the USA attempted to reduce its deficit? The USA still accounts for almost 50 per cent of OECD output and is, for example, the UK's and Japan's largest single market. Therefore a decline in economic activity in the USA is likely to have a profound impact upon other countries. Cutting government spending sharply, everything else being equal, would be deflationary. One result would be a fall in demand for imports in the USA. Another might be a fall in the value of the US dollar and hence an increase in the competitiveness of US exports in world markets. This could occur if the administration attempted to minimize the overall deflationary effects of the budget reduction by loosening monetary policy and bringing down interest rates. The extent to which such events would affect other economies and firms outside the USA depends, of course, upon the wider impact of these changes upon the world economy. Would, for example, interest rates fall worldwide in response to a cut in the USA? What is clear is that firms exporting to the USA have profited in the 1980s because of a relatively strong dollar and buoyant US demand. A major deflation in the US to correct the twin deficits could throw all of this into reverse.

Questions

1. What measures could the US government take to correct the budget deficit? Consider the demand-side and supply-side effects of your recommendations.

2. Consider more fully the likely impact of reducing the US budget deficit on the US economy and the world economy.

6 Linkages between money, output, prices and interest rates

In the UK, monetary policy has dominated the debate concerning macroeconomic policy since the mid-1970s and right through the 1980s. Increasingly, however, economists are becoming more and more sceptical about the linkages between growth in the money supply, the growth in output and inflation. The question at the forefront of the debate today concerns whether or not increases in the stock of money in circulation can lead to an increase in the economy's real output and hence reduce unemployment, or do they simply result in higher inflation?

Since the announcement of monetary targets was made public in 1976 as part of an IMF loan agreement, control over the money supply has been at the heart of the UK government's attempts to reduce inflationary pressures. This single premise has formed the nucleus of the so-called medium-term financial strategy implemented by the Conservatives at the start of the 1980s. Interest rates have been used as the key policy instrument in this respect (see Chapter 6).

Table 10.5 reports data on the UK's money supply, output, inflation and the rate of interest for the period 1976–88.

Questions

1. Outline the theoretical foundations for the argument that control over the growth in the money supply should reduce inflationary pressures.

2. Using the data shown in Table 10.5, graph and examine the relationship between:

   (a) The rate of growth of M0 and the rate of growth of prices (i.e. inflation).

   (b) The rate of growth of M3 and inflation.

   What difference does it make if inflation is plotted against the rate of growth of M0 and M3 two years previous and why might it make sense to do this?

3. Examine the hypothesis that monetary growth causes increases in real output in the short-run.

Table 10.5 Money, output, inflation and interest rates

	MO[a] (£m)	M3[a] (£m)	Output[b] (GDP, £m) current prices	Prices[c] (GDP deflator) 1985 = 100	Interest rates[d] (yield on Treasury bills)
1976	7,626	39,111	112,571	43.0	13.98
1977	8,495	42,704	129,618	48.2	6.39
1978	9,751	49,272	149,553	54.0	11.91
1979	11,013	55,340	173,235	61.0	16.49
1980	11,635	65,536	201,097	72.3	13.58
1981	11,863	82,537	218,838	79.5	15.39
1982	12,251	89,878	238,318	85.2	9.96
1983	13,043	99,851	261,217	90.0	9.04
1984	13,789	109,904	280,227	94.9	9.33
1985	14,425	124,481	306,849	100.0	11.49
1986	15,159	150,135	326,433	102.7	10.94
1987	15,894	184,507	358,270	107.8	8.38
1988	17,169	214,970*	400,029	114.7	12.91

[a] End-period, amount outstanding: seasonally adjusted (* third quarter).
[b] Average estimates of GDP (expenditure-based) at factor cost.
[c] Implied GDP deflator based on expenditure data at factor cost.
[d] Average discount rate expressed as the rate at which interest is earned during the life of the bills.
Source: Economic Trends (London: HMSO).

4. How sensitive are changes in the money supply (M0 or M3) to changes in interest rates (yield on Treasury bills)?

5. Comment, in general, on the empirical strength of the monetarist economic strategy.

7 Outlook for the economy

Below is a commentary, written at the end of 1989, on the state of the UK economy. It covers a broad range of macroeconomic indicators and provides an overview of the various problems faced by the UK government at that time with regard to management of the economy. This case study, therefore, is 'all-embracing' in that it makes reference to the key economic variables that have been introduced in this book. At the end of the case study there is a collection of questions that test understanding of the macroeconomy.

In late October 1989 Mr Nigel Lawson resigned as the UK Chancellor of the Exchequer over sharp differences with the Prime Minister on the desirability of the early entry of sterling into the EMS Exchange Rate Mechanism [see case study 2]. Three weeks later his successor Mr John Major had the unenviable task of presenting the government's Autumn Financial Statement, an occasion when government forecasts for the economy are revised and public spending targets for the next three years are revealed.

A period of rapid economic growth which saw the UK near the head of the economic growth league in Europe, triggered rising inflation and a severe deterioration in the balance of payments on current account by 1988. In an attempt to stem the explosion in consumer credit, which lay behind the surge in imports, from June 1988 short-term interest rates in Britain were raised gradually from $7\frac{1}{2}$ to 15 per cent. Against this background it was expected that the Treasury's predictions for the economy would be gloomy. And so they were, exceeding in pessimism the forecasts of most City economists. With Treasury forecasts suggesting a sharp slowdown of economic growth in 1990, stagnant domestic demand but inflation staying above 7 per cent to the middle of the year and falling only to 5.75 per cent by its end, and a balance of payments deficit declining only to £15bn, the Chancellor predicted that 1990 may not be an easy year. Forecasts for all of the major economic variables have worsened not only since the 1988 Autumn Financial Statement but since the budget the previous March. Comparisons are given in Table 10.6. In particular, the balance of payments deficit and the inflation rate are now expected to exceed the forecasts made last March for the end of 1989 until well into 1991.

The need to maintain high interest rates means that the Treasury now predicts a miserly 1.25 per cent real growth in GDP next year, compared with 2 per cent in 1989 and over 4 per cent in 1988. Leaving out the oil sector, the projection is even bleaker with only a 0.75 per cent expansion in the remainder of the economy, compared with 5 per cent in 1988 and around 3 per cent in 1989. At the same time, there is to be a sharp fall in the rate of growth of consumer spending. Consumer spending is expected to decline from a heady 6.75 per cent growth in real terms in 1988 and 3.75 per cent in 1989 to a mere 1.25 per cent in 1990. Business investment is also expected to react to the economic slowdown. A 30 per cent real increase in business investment between 1986 and 1988 is expected to give way to a modest 4.5 per cent rise in 1990. Alongside this, private investment in dwellings is also declining (the housing market is currently bearing the brunt of the squeeze on the economy). The growth in total fixed investment by business, private dwellings and central government is expected, therefore, to fall from 13.25 per cent in 1988 to

Table 10.6 Economic performance and forecasts[a]

	March 1988 forecast for 1988	1988 outturn	March budget forecast for 1989	Latest Treasury forecast for 1989	Treasury forecast for 1990	Average error of forecasts[b]
Economic growth (GDP) % change	3.0	4.25	2.5	2.0	1.25	1.0
Consumer spending % change	4.0	6.75	3.5	3.75	1.25	1.25
Government current spending (central and local government) % change	1.0	0.5	0.5	−0.25	0.25	0.5
Private and public investment % change	6.5	13.25	4.5	5.25	1.75	3.25
Stockbuilding change as % GDP	0	0.75	−0.5	0.5	−1.5	0.75
Exports % change	3.0	0.75	4.5	4.75	6.25	1.75
Imports % change	6.5	12.25	4.5	9.25	1.25	3.25
Balance of payments current account £bn	−4.0	−14.5	−11.0	−20.0	−15.0	5.75
PSBR £bn[c]	−3.0	−14.5	−14.0	−12.5	—	3.25
Retail price index (inflation 4th quarter to 4th quarter) % change	4.0	6.5	5.5	7.25	5.75	2.0
Rise in total spending (money GDP) % change	7.5	10.75	8.0	8.5	6.75	1.5

[a] All figures are percentages and at constant prices except where indicated.

[b] The errors relate to average differences (on either side of the central figure) between autumn forecasts and outturns over the last ten years.

[c] Public sector borrowing requirement, negative indicates debt repayment (budget surplus).

Sources: Autumn Financial Statement; *Financial Times,* 16 November 1989.

5.25 per cent in 1989 and only 1.75 per cent in 1990. Such figures imply that the British economy is precariously close to an economic recession.

How long the economy must be restrained by a tight monetary policy depends upon how long it takes to bring inflation and the balance of payments deficit down. Although the government's narrow definition of money, M0, came back in September 1989 to within the 0–5 per cent target range set in that year's March budget, the wider definition of money, M4, continues to grow at around 18 per cent, despite evidence of a slowdown in the expansion of consumer credit. M4 may or may not matter – the government obviously prefers to use M0 for official targeting purposes. But the prospects for an early cut in interest rates remain bleak. At present, production needs to be switched to export markets and imports must be curbed.

Since 1985, export volume has risen by 25 per cent but import volume by 50 per cent, turning a UK surplus on current account of over £3bn in 1985 into an expected deficit of £20bn in 1989. To bring the deficit down to £15bn in 1990 requires the growth in the volume of non-oil imports to fall from 10.25 per cent in 1989 to 2.25 per cent in 1990. At the same time, the growth in export volume will have to rise from 0.75 per cent in 1988 to 6.25 per cent in 1990.

With slower growth than expected and pressure from the spending ministries for more government spending, the Chancellor revealed that the government was unwilling to try and hold public spending for the current financial year to within previously agreed limits. The Chancellor added about £5bn to previous spending plans for 1990/1, an act which was widely welcomed in some parts of the media as evidence of a more pragmatic attitude to public spending, though it received a more cautious response in the City.

Public spending will now increase by 2.1 per cent in real terms in the 1990/1 financial year beginning in April, based upon the government's estimate of inflation as measured by the retail price index (RPI). Consequently, public expenditure as a percentage of GDP (net of privatization proceeds) will rise marginally from 38.75 to 39 per cent, the first such rise since the 1984/5 fiscal year. The state's share of economic activity remains at its lowest proportion for over twenty years and the public finances remain healthy with a predicted budget surplus of £12.5bn in 1989/90. Nevertheless, the government's policy of cutting public spending as a proportion of GDP has been given a jolt.

It remains the government's intention to continue its tax cutting programme, hoping to reduce the basic rate of income tax (the rate paid by around 93 per cent of income tax payers) from 25 to 20 per cent before the next general election. But the new Chancellor added a hint of caution:

'I will certainly make tax reductions when and if I think it is prudent to do so, and not before'.

Whether it can ever be prudent to make tax cuts which fuel consumer spending when the balance of payments is in deficit and the inflation rate exceeds that of trading competitors must remain a moot point. The tax cuts in the 1988 budget contributed to the current economic crisis. Meanwhile, Mr Major, when challenged, did not rule out tax increases to dampen economic activity further should they be considered necessary – though such an act would be a great embarrassment to what professes to be a tax-cutting administration.

The Chancellor completed his Autumn Financial Statement to the House of Commons on an up-beat note:

> The economy enters the 1990s in incomparably better shape than it entered the 1980s. The supply-side reforms of the last decade have left business and industry better able to handle both the short-term difficulties before us and the longer-term opportunities to come. I have no doubt that we must stick to the policies that have turned the British economy around. And that we are determined to do.

A return to what appears to be uncomfortably similar to the old stop–go cycles of the 1960s and 1970s – with fast growth triggering inflation and balance of payments crises leading to deflation – may not have jarred Mr Major's faith in what has been achieved since 1979. But some more objective observers are less sanguine. Even the trumpeted public spending increases will only produce the expected real rise in services if inflation in these programmes is limited to the figures forecast. The recent failure to predict inflation accurately, alongside growing demands from public sector workers for higher wages, threatens even this outcome.

Questions

1. Explain why 'a period of rapid economic growth' triggered rising inflation and a severe deterioration in the balance of payments on current account in 1988?

2. High interest rates are clearly intended to bring about 'a sharp fall in consumer spending'. What costs and benefits can be expected from this, assuming that the policy works?

3. What factors may delay any improvement in the balance of payments position?

4. Some commentators have argued that interest rates are being used by the government not just to influence the demand side of the economy, but also the supply side. Explain how a high interest rate policy might have supply-side implications, both positive and negative in effect.

5. Why was the announcement of an addition of £5bn to public spending plans for 1990/1 given 'a cautious response by the City'?

6. In what ways can it be argued that 'the tax cuts in the 1988 budget contributed to the current economic crisis'?

7. The government professes to be a tax-cutting administration. What rationale lies behind this standpoint?

Appendix: Sources of economic data for managers

This appendix gives details of the principal sources of UK economic data as well as the key international sources of data. The UK data are categorized according to the following headings:

1. General.
2. Economic growth.
3. Personal income and saving.
4. Industry and commerce.
5. Labour statistics.
6. Inflation.
7. Housing and construction.
8. Money, banking and finance.
9. The balance of payments.

Two useful guides to UK statistical sources are available:

1. *Government Statistics: A brief guide to sources* (London: Information Services Division, Cabinet Office). (free)
2. CSO, *Guide to Official Statistics* (London: HMSO, occasional).

UK sources

1. General

Annual Abstract of Statistics, HMSO.
Bank of England Quarterly Bulletin, Bank of England.
Economic Progress Report, H.M. Treasury. Monthly.
Economic Trends, HMSO. Monthly and annual supplement.
Financial Statistics, HMSO. Monthly.
Monthly Digest of Statistics, HMSO.
UK National Accounts, HMSO. Annually.
Regional Trends, HMSO. Annually.
Social Trends, HMSO. Annually.

2. Economic growth

Economic Trends, tables 6, 8, 26, 28, 68–71. Special section January, April, July and October.
Monthly Digest of Statistics, tables 1.1–1.3, 7.1.
UK National Accounts, sections 1–3.

3. Personal income and saving

Economic Trends, tables 10, 12, 14.
Financial Statistics, section 9.
Monthly Digest of Statistics, tables 1.5, 14.1, 14.2.
UK National Accounts, section 4.

4. Industry and commerce

Business Monitor MA3, Business Statistics Office. Annually.
Economic Trends, tables 16, 18, 22, 60, 62.
Financial Statistics, section 8.
Monthly Digest of Statistics, tables 1.7–1.9.
UK National Accounts, section 5.

5. Labour statistics

Economic Trends, tables 34, 36, 38, 40.
Employment Gazette, HMSO. Monthly.
New Earnings Survey, HMSO. Annually.
Monthly Digest of Statistics, section 3.

6. Inflation

Economic Trends, tables 5, 42.
Employment Gazette, tables 6.1–6.7.
Family Expenditure Survey, Department of Employment, HMSO. Annually.
Monthly Digest of Statistics, tables 18.1–18.6.
Price Index Numbers for Current Cost Accounting, HMSO (annually) and *Business Monitor MM17*, HMSO (monthly) for producer price indices.

7. Housing and construction

Housing and Construction Statistics, HMSO. Annually.

8. Money, banking and finance

Abstract of Banking Statistics, City of London and Scottish Banks (CLSB). Annually.
Bank of England Quarterly Bulletin, Statistical annex.
Economic Trends, tables 52, 54, 56, 64, 66.
Financial Statistics, sections 3, 6, 7, 11.
BSA Bulletin, Building Societies Association; now *Housing Finance*, Council of Mortgage Lenders. Quarterly.

9. The balance of payments

Bank of England Quarterly Bulletin, statistical annex, sections 14–18, 'External balance sheet of the UK', annual article, September or August issue.
British Council for Invisible Exports, *Annual Report*.
Economic Trends, tables 46, 48, 50, and quarterly balance of payments article in March, June, September and December issues.
Financial Statistics, section 10 and tables 13.1–13.3.
Monthly Review of External Trade Statistics, and *Annual Supplement*, DTI.
The Overseas Trade Statistics of the United Kingdom, HMSO. Monthly and annually.
Overseas Trade Analysed in Terms of Industries, Business Monitor MQ10, HMSO. Quarterly.
The United Kingdom Balance of Payments (Pink Book), HMSO. Annually.

International sources

General

UN Statistical Year Book and *UN National Accounts Statistics*, United Nations (UN), New York. Annually.
Yearbook of Labour Statistics, International Labour Organization (ILO), Geneva. Annually.
International Financial Statistics, International Monetary Fund (IMF), Washington. Monthly.
National Accounts, Organization for Economic Co-operation and Development (OECD), Paris. Annually.

EC

A wide range of statistics publications is published by the Statistical Office of the European Communities (SOEC) in Luxembourg. Selected titles are given below:

Basic Statistics of the Community. Annually.
Industry: Statistical yearbook.
Industrial Trends: Monthly statistics.
Industrial Production: Quarterly statistics.
Structure and Activity of Industry. Annually.
Earnings: Industry and services. Half-yearly.
Labour Force Survey. Annually.
National Accounts, 3 volumes. Annually.
External Trade: Statistical yearbook. Annually.

A full listing of EC statistical sources is available in *Eurostat Catalogue*, free from Eurostat and from the Office of Official Publications of the European Communities, Luxembourg.

Further reading

There are many books which provide further in-depth treatment of the aspects of macroeconomic theory and policy reviewed in this book. Most, however, are intended for serious students of economics and require some previous grounding in economic theory. The following have been selected because they build upon the contents of this book yet are intelligible to the economics non-specialist.

Chrystal, K. A., *Controversies in Macroeconomics*, 2nd edn (Oxford: Philip Allan, 1983).

Donaldson, P. and Farquhar, J., *Understanding the British Economy* (Harmondsworth: Penguin, 1988).

Johnson, C., *Measuring the Economy* (London: Macmillan, 1988).

Kay, J.A. and King, M.A., *The British Tax System*, 5th edn (Oxford: Oxford University Press, 1990).

Keegan, W., *Mrs Thatcher's Economic Experiment* (Harmondsworth: Penguin, 1984).

Likierman, A., *Public Expenditure: The public spending process* (Harmondsworth: Penguin, 1988).

Pratten, C., *Applied Macroeconomics* (Oxford: Oxford University Press, 1985).

Robinson, P., *The Unbalanced Recovery* (Oxford: Philip Allan, 1988).

Shaw, G.K., *Keynesian Economics: The permanent revolution* (Aldershot: Edward Elgar, 1988).

Vane, H.R. and Thompson, J.L., *An Introduction to Macroeconomic Policy*, 2nd edn (Brighton: Wheatsheaf Books, 1985).

Index